This book is dedicated to God, the author of my soul.

In Appreciation

Bestselling author, Dorothea Benton Frank, often writes lengthy, wordy acknowledgments in her books. After she finished writing a six-page "thank you" in her novel, Pawleys Island, her last sentence reads, "So shoot me. I'm sentimental, and I don't care who knows it."

When you write a book of essays about life, there are a lot of folks to thank. Without these extraordinary people, there would be no stories to tell. So, don't shoot me!

David Gendusa, words cannot express how much I thank you for your patience with this temperamental girl. When I told you I wanted to start a new career as a writer, you never questioned me. Your humor, your strength, your girls Kimberly Gendusa and Kristin Mascari, and your crazy Italian/New Orleans ways have warmed my heart and completed my life for thirteen special years.

My children, Amy Lockman, Heather Nystrum, and Corey Lockman, you are my three amazing blessings. Your support and love are beyond measure, and there are not enough words to tell you how much you are adored and appreciated. I am honored to be your "Mom." There would be no pages without you.

To have a granddaughter like you, Avery, lights my world and fills my heart. You are a beautiful person with a sweet spirit and a wicked sense of humor. You will grace other's lives with joy as you go through life just as you have mine. Never change.

Carter Mae Mascari and Jaxon Fender, even though you are only two years old, you have brought such happiness and laughter to our lives we cannot imagine our world without you.

Mike Nystrum and Michael Mascari, you know I warned you both about me as a mom-in-law, so thanks for hanging in there and loving my fried chicken!

My most humble thanks to my parents, Ray and Elizabeth

Walker, my grandparents John and Nannie Pugh, Robert and Rose Walker, my great-grandmother, Mollie Randolph Sparks, and all the cousins, aunts, and uncles, who comprise my family. You all have given me an abundance of tales to tell and more love than one can imagine.

To my brother, John Walker, you were the guardian of my soul, and even though you don't live on earth with me any longer, you still are. Your wife Patricia and children, Emily Schneller and David Walker, plus all your grandchildren, warm my heart just as you always did. Alex, Austin, Samantha, Noah, and Benjamin keep you alive until I can see you again.

Deborah Kerr, you have read every word I ever wrote, know every thought I ever had, and amazingly understand them all! If God had not plopped me down in the house next to yours, I sincerely doubt this book would exist. You are one of the dearest people in the world and those of us who call you friend, mother, grandmother, sister, and aunt are blessed. Thank you, my sweet soul sister.

Richie Mahaffey, from the time we were fifteen, you have been the constant light in my life. I guess God knew I would need a special brother, so he blessed me with you. No matter how many miles and days we spend apart, you and I know we are always together.

The LaGrange High School Class of 1965 is a beautiful group of people whom I will love until the day I die. Where would I be without all of you? Your prayers for my family, your outpouring of love and support require more thanks than mere words can express. When I have written stories about you, I hope I expressed just how special you are in my heart.

Friends are many, and I can't possibly list all, but I would like to sincerely thank Ricki Vann, The Encourager, whose belief in me prompted me to believe, and Michele Thomas, The Planner, whose wise counsel and knowledge makes me a bit wiser. Many kudos to Geri Harkins, The Inspirer, who gives a whole new meaning to "Steel Magnolia" and "Southern Belle."

To all my extraordinary friends in Brookside, you are the best!

A special thanks to my amigos John Wade Freeman and Whit Fackler who told me to write from my heart and I listened. Marie Daniel Hardy, Jo Taylor Payne, Ree Boatwright Edwards are the "Ladies Who Lunched" and how special it is to know sometimes, friends do last forever.

Thanks to long time pals forever, Lori Deuben and Shirley Carter. Krista Cadenhead, I know you are an angel in heaven now just like you were here with me. Roberta Love, you saved me many times from myself and I will always be grateful for your friendship.

Kay and Joe Dye, you are an inspiration to all those who know you. I can't tell you how many times you have lifted my spirits.

To my design clients and friends who walked through my world during my long career and listened to my stories and told me to write them down…I thank you.

So much gratitude goes to Daniel Evans, Matthew Strother, Jim Boone and all of *LaGrange Daily News* for allowing me to spill my heart in your paper every Thursday. Thank you.

Allison St. Claire and Lee Walburn…I owe you! WOW! You sent me tons of courage to go forward with this book. Allison, thank you for giving me the opportunity to spread my words across the country. Lee, thank you for your excellent book, *Just My Type*, and for finding Dekie Hicks and Michaele Flynn Prince who have made these pages become something which once existed only in my dreams.

Thank you to the countless readers who take a moment to read my work. This book belongs to you. I love you all!

Lynn

Introduction

Over three years ago, I learned a valuable lesson: Life isn't over until they call your name from way up yonder!

When I was a girl I always dreamed of writing and thought, "Someday the stories whirling in my head will find there way into sentences that will spill onto paper."

Life stalled my dream when reality meant raising and providing for my children, so they could pursue their own dreams. After retiring from a career in Interior Design, God began to whisper and then He yelled, "Time to put the stories on paper, Lynn!"

I was excited when my first essay was published, and more amazed when I became a weekly newspaper columnist, and astounded when my columns spread nationwide. After writing for a few months, a dear friend sent me a note which said, "Lynn, always write from your heart." I hope you find I have done so.

These pages are filled with words from my soul and with my truth. I know fried chicken is magical, America is beautiful, families are gifts, and good friends are angels. I believe homemade is better than store-bought, healing takes time, lessons are priceless, Christmas is pure joy, age is a state of mind, and death is a chance to live a new life through faith.

As you walk through the chapters, may you see your own story written within the words. I hope you take away the knowledge that no matter what you may endure, life still goes on until the final chapter when you hear your name from way up yonder. Until then, live boldly, beautifully, and benevolently.

Contents

Friends

Shadows

Southland

Healing

Age(less)

Lessons

Treasures

America

Celebrate

Joy

The Last Chapter

There is nothing to writing. All you do is sit down at a typewriter and bleed.

—*Ernest Hemingway*

Family

The family is the heart of who we are. We often take those closest to us for granted, but with time and wisdom, we learn that family is the greatest of God's many gifts.

Those who live life by our side or those who have made a path before us are treasures more valuable than silver or gold.

When we welcome a new baby, watch a child grow, weep over the loss of a loved one, or rejoice at a reunion, we understand love's deep and abiding nature.

I was blessed beyond measure to be a part of a family whose members bring smiles, tears, and a sense of forever to my soul. They are the center of my universe and the ribbon around my heart.

A Journey To Forever

Today is Mother's Day. I am on my computer writing to you in the quiet hours of a Sunday morning in May, and I am happy. I am thankful for the hours to put my heart on paper and not to cry my heart out for a Mom who is no longer here, and for children who are far away.

My daughter Amy is in California running a race at Disneyland in Anaheim. I am glad she is taking a vacation to see friends and is happily doing something she loves.

My daughter Heather is at home in Florida relaxing with her daughter and husband. They will probably go to the beach today and celebrate life. Heather has always loved the ocean which both calms and gives her great joy.

My son is settling into his new home in Colorado. I am sure he is preparing for another trip to South Africa to save the beautiful animals of our world. Corey has always tried to "save" something all his life.

I am the happiest Mom on the planet. I am grateful God decided to give these three children to this undeserving girl. I am glad they are all doing something they love.

When I was in high school, I dreamed of a white house with the proverbial picket fence to hold my family of six children and a great husband. I would sew their clothes, prepare their meals and have hot cookies for them when they arrived home from school.

I never saw myself as a career woman or a woman who would celebrate some holidays not surrounded by a gaggle of kids. That was not me.

Then life happened. I did marry a great guy, had trouble

having those six children, and lived in an apartment for years. More years passed and life upended again.

Divorced, alone, with three children, and a career. Motherhood was not only a blessing but a hardship. I look back on those days and wonder how in the world I did it all. I would wake at 5:30, cook breakfast, get the children ready for school, then off to work until dark. Back home, I would cook dinner, clean house, wash clothes and read a bedtime story or three.

I struggled financially, had horrible child care, broke down a couple of times from sheer exhaustion, battled depression, and prayed a lot.

In other words, I was one of the thousands of women going through the same thing. We tried to do it all. It was virtually impossible to do it alone. My extended family lived in other states. My three little ones were my only constant lifeline to life.

Would I do it all again? You bet! Was it hard? Yep! I was so busy providing I know I didn't do it all correctly. I was by no means the best mother. I was selfish at times; I cried too much at times, and I know I yelled too many times. I disciplined too harshly or too leniently. I struggled the whole way, but there is one thing I did perfectly. I loved those children with every fiber of my being, and they knew it.

My children gave me the bold courage to try anything. They gave me energy when I thought it depleted. They gave me laughter when my cheeks were drenched in tears. They gave me hope when all I had left was a prayer. They gave me friendship and companionship when I felt alone. They gave me honor as a human being.

All three children grew and worked hard to help finance their education. They believed in God. They loved one another. They survived their teenage years and my teenaged mind.

My children have crossed many hurdles in life. They have done so with pure guts and determination. They understand that life can change on a dime and that living is a gift never to be taken for granted.

I am thankful I have been there in crisis to hold their hands and encourage them. I know I am capable of heroic feats that without them I would have never accomplished.

I have learned that my youthful dreams of bliss could not hold a candle to the reality of this life, this love, this day, this moment.

Even though I will not see my children this Mother's Day, I can look at their faces in framed photographs which hang on the wall above my desk. I realize it is those children, along with God's grace, that provided my finest hours.

There is Corey in his baseball uniform at age five beaming with pride. Heather with her big blue eyes, staring down at me with a slight, sad smile at age two. Amy, with her curly hair at age one, being held in my arms and laughing because I am tickling her leg.

There in the corner is my mother at age 86, holding her great-granddaughter. The loves of my life in snapshot moments of living.

I hope wherever you are today; you take a moment to thank God for your Mother, your child, your grandchild, and all those in your family and realize that these blessings are your journey to forever.

top to bottom
Lynn, Amy,
Heather, Corey
1981

front row L to R: Kendra Curtis, Kimberly Gendusa, Kristin Mascari, Lynn Gendusa, Heather Nystrum, Avery Nystrum in front, Amy Lockman
back row L to R: Corey Lockman, Ryan Fender, Michael Mascari, David Gendusa, Mike Nystrum

Jaxon Fender & Carter Mae Mascari

Her Name Was "Grandpa"

How do you love a child? How do you become the memory that makes someone smile forever? Does your life exemplify your good beliefs and encourage children to follow you?

The greatest gift we have as adults is children in our lives. It doesn't matter if we are a parent, grandparent, aunt, uncle, or a friend of a child. To love a child and have the love returned is the blessing that is beyond all the riches in the world. Period.

My brother John was three and watching his favorite grandmother make biscuits. He watched as the flour hit the dough board and dusted the air. She was talking to him the whole time and laughed as the white powder settled on his eyelashes.

John had been having a lot of trouble with the name "Grandma." Since he was born with six grandmothers he would get them confused easily. Two great, great grandmothers, two great grandmothers, and two grandmothers all living in the same town! He was the first grandchild. It was asking too much for him to remember them all. Even though John had six grandmothers, he only had one living grandfather.

Suddenly, while standing beside his grandmother in her kitchen, he came up with a solution.

His coal brown eyes opened wide as he tugged his grandmother's apron, "You gonna be Grandpa!"

"John, I am Grandma and he is your Granddaddy," she replied, as she pointed to her husband.

"You Grandpa and he Granddaddy!" he emphatically stated again. Then he walked away.

From that moment on, nine grandchildren and eighteen great grandchildren would forever call her Grandpa.

The name would also be representative of unconditional love. A love that allowed her to be called whatever these children wanted to call her.

Many people have crossed my path in life, but without question, I have never known anyone quite like Grandpa.

She didn't just say, "I love you;" she showed it in countless ways. There was nothing she loved more than children. For those of us who were in her life, we all knew that to be fact. When she played or talked with us, she became our age. She even let us play with the wrinkles on her hand, and make fun of her false teeth until she got new ones. She laughed at herself and was never embarrassed by any of us.

I can recall being in her small home with many of my cousins. Grandpa would play games with us all day, fish with us, tell us stories, and stay up way past her bedtime.

Then right before she went to her room to join my sleeping grandfather, she would sit at the end of the hall and read her Bible. That is how she made us understand the concept of priorities.

When she played games, she would never let any of us undeservedly win. By doing so she taught us to have the grace to lose and understand the word fairness.

Her garden bloomed in July with white gladiolas that reached up to the sun. She always wanted white because they were pure and heavenly. She taught us that out of dirt, toil, and care comes beauty.

We all stayed with Grandpa many times. She would make sure she had everyone's favorite food in the house. She would cook until her old apron was soiled and dark. She taught us we were each special in someone's eyes

It is hard for me to write all that she was and did in her 97 years on earth. I could fill the whole book with words and stories about this remarkable, kind human being.

Her laughter fills my heart today. Her hands calm my soul and lift me up. Her spirit still wraps me in unconditional love and comfort.

We bring children into our world hoping they will be perfect and wonderful. I think instead we need to be as close as possible to wonderful and perfect for them. To make a child feel loved unconditionally, feel special, feel like we would rather be with them than anything else, is honoring the gift that was given to us in the first place.

Years ago, I could not decide what to give Grandpa for Christmas. So instead of a gift, I decided to write a story about her and send it to her county paper in Tennessee. The newspaper printed the story using the entire second page of the paper. The title in bold lettering was, "MERRY CHRISTMAS GRANDPA!"

The name my brother had given her all those years ago was now a bold headline and that was as it should be.

For children to grow up with adults who make us a headline in their hearts, giving us a love that will never die long after we are gone, is the greatest blessing we will give them and ourselves.

"And her children will arise up and call her blessed" were the words on a cross-stitched sampler hanging above Grandpa's bed when she left this earth. No truer words were ever written.

Nancy Melissa Pugh (Nannie/Grandpa) maternal grandmother circa 1950

The Banana Pudding On The Window Sill

The car pulled onto the dirt and pebble drive, passed Granddaddy's lumber mill and slowly wrapped around the little fishing pond. My mother would apply the brakes, stopping just shy of my grandparent's carport.

Like many houses in the Tennessee hills, the carport was never used for cars. Instead it was to house the gliders, chairs, and plants accompanied by a big braided rug covering the concrete. This outside haven of mental warmth was for watermelon feast, playing board games in the fresh air, as well as being the welcome station for all guests.

My summer vacations always began with a two week stay at my Grandpa's house on the Cumberland Plateau in Tennessee.

Those days spent with my grandparents were the highlight of every summer. And, every June upon my arrival, sitting on the window sill was my favorite: a cooling banana pudding.

Homemade lard biscuits with homemade grape jelly, fresh cured pork tenderloins, fried fresh fish, pot roast and garden vegetables were just some of the treats that adorned my plate every day. When the cousins came to visit and play, Grandpa made sure the refrigerator contained the favorite dessert and drink for each one.

"Why do you cook as much as you do, Grandpa?" I would ask.

"Well, honey, that's one way I show love," she would say as she wiped her floured hands on her apron.

Grandpa would rise on Sundays at 4 a.m. She would start to cook pot roast and fried chicken, plus prepare the side dishes before we all left for church.

"Why do you have to get up so early?" I would question.

"Well, honey, it's because I need to get to church to give love to God," she would answer as she untied her apron.

For all of us who were blessed to call her our grandmother or great grandmother, there is not one who doubted her love for us or God, ever.

Mikey is turning seventy this month. Mikey and his wife are our friends down the street. We gathered, along with three other couples, for a little birthday celebration in the mountains just north of Atlanta. I asked his wife, Ricki, what kind of cake Mikey would like for me to bake for his birthday.

"He likes pies. But don't go to the trouble. No one is eating sweets these days!" Ricki responded.

"What kind of pie does he like?" I asked, ignoring the statement about eating sweets.

"Chocolate and key lime," she finally said, knowing I was oblivious to her objections.

Everyone who knows me, knows you will not stop me from making a dessert. I put on my apron, get my flour out, and generally make a mess, just like my Grandpa. While I stood in my kitchen stirring the chocolate and grating lime zest, I felt my grandmother's spirit, as I always do while cooking or baking something special.

All the friends who accompanied us, including my own husband, thought me foolish for making the two pies that Mikey loved. They all thought the pies would not be eaten. "No one is eating sweets these days," they declared. I chose to ignore their foolishness.

I put three candles in each pie and handed them to Mikey as the group sang the birthday song. His eyes lit up when I told him one was Key Lime topped with peaked meringue and the other, Chocolate Cream, with the same fluffy topping.

It was funny how all those folks who don't eat sweets anymore were fighting over the last pieces. Not a crumb was left in either pie plate.

Mikey called me a few days later.

"Lynn, those pies were fantastic! I can't tell you how much I appreciated the trouble and the time you took to make my birthday very special."

My Grandpa taught me a valuable lesson all those years ago. When you care for someone, you must show that you do. It is not just in the words, it is in the trouble. It is not only in making pies, but in going the extra mile to make someone feel special and loved.

My granddaughter comes to visit me every summer. I always have her favorite foods in the house. She is now almost twelve, and has become a fantastic little baker. She loves making special treats for her family and friends while wiping her floured hands on her handmade apron.

One day, when she was very young, I had her favorite food on the counter when she arrived for her summer visit.

"Grandma, why do you like to cook so much?" she questioned.

"Well, it's my way to show how much I love you," I replied as she stared at the banana pudding waiting for her.

Grandpa's precious love lives on.

The Finest Athlete I Ever Knew

Dedicated to Elizabeth Pugh Walker 7/20/1919 – 6/27/2010

It was around 1934 when a tall, skinny fifteen-year-old girl traveled down the mountain to Murfreesboro, Tennessee. The road was curvy and treacherous as most roads were in those days.

She tightly held the basketball in her lap as her father drove her toward the town that was three hours away. After they parked the car, she was quiet and a bit nervous as she approached the gym were the Tennessee Mid-State Free Throw Championship was to commence.

Dark hair framed her pretty, delicate face, but behind her chestnut eyes hid a fierce competitor. Not only was she highly competitive, but more importantly, she also believed that "she could."

She positioned the toes of her white high tops up to the free throw line and dribbled the ball for a moment. She took a deep breath as she threw the first ball and watched it swoosh through the hoop.

She would sink 48 out of 50 free throws that day and walk away with the championship.

Lesson Learned: Always believe in your own ability.

The car ambled back up the mountain to the little town of Monterey. That same year she, along with her best friend, Violet, would lead their high school team to victory and claim the Tennessee Mid-State Basketball Championship.

Lesson Learned: Always be a team player.

Within a year, she would start to play tennis. Her methodical play and competitive nature forged her into a solid champion of tennis. None of her peers could beat her. A picture of her holding her racket, dressed in white, on the court was back in the hometown paper.

She graduated from high school at the age of fifteen. She was the class Valedictorian and voted "Most Athletic."

Lesson Learned: Intelligence combined with practice make a great champion.

The years would pass and for a while, the world of sport was replaced with babies, bottles, and caring for others. Every now and then, she would pick up a ball or swing a racket.

One day, at age 40, she declared she was going to learn to play golf.

Her children asked, "Mom, aren't you a little too old to learn a new sport?" They forgot whom they were talking to.

This ancient mother won two club championships by the time she was 45 years old.

Lesson Learned: One is never too old to start something new.

She would play golf until she was in her early eighties. Then one day sports were over, and her life was never quite the same.

After she broke her hip at 89, she required rehabilitation. It was difficult for her to absorb the reality that her frail body was failing her. Depression set in. One afternoon while in rehab, her physical therapist handed her a basketball after she noticed the dark eyes of her patient staring at the orange ball in the corner.

The physical therapist placed the ball in her lap while she was sitting in the wheelchair. Immediately, the former champion picked up the ball and threw it accurately into the arms of her amazed therapist. They played daily until the depression lifted and the hip healed.

Lesson Learned: The body may fall, but the spirit within can lift you up.

Within a year, the last days of her life were upon her. The elderly athlete was a mere shadow of her former self. Her fierceness was gone. She was ready to go to her eternal home.

On a Sunday night in late June 2010, I took this woman's

hand into mine. Her eyes were closed as I whispered in her ear, "Mother, I don't know if you can hear me, but go on to Heaven. Run like the wind, and don't look back."

I had walked away from Mom's bedside for a few minutes, when the Hospice nurse ran toward me.

"Miss Lynn, your mother has passed! I have been working with hospice for 25 years and I have never seen anything like this! Your mother was hot and perspiring as if she had been running when she took her last breath!

Through my tears, somewhere was a smile in my heart.

Lesson Learned: Life continues and living returns.

When I reach Heaven, I will quickly recognize my mother. She will be the one coming toward me holding a basketball, tennis racquet, or a golf club.

"You ready to play?" she asks.

"Yes, Mom, but I forgot to tell you something before you ran home."

"What is that?" She looks puzzled.

"Mom, you were the best coach and the finest athlete I ever knew."

Elizabeth Pugh holding basketball, Tennessee College basketball team, 1937

The Greatest Of Fathers

My father, Ray Walker, was only five years old when his father passed away. He would often tell me, "Lynn, I don't know how to be a good father because I never was raised by one." A statement which always made me sad.

Yes, Dad did struggle at times being a Dad, but then again, I struggled at times being a daughter. Sometimes, being a good father is not about being perfect, but being perfectly human.

Daddy, along with two older brothers and a sister, was raised by a strong woman. It wasn't an easy life, but what it developed in Daddy was a powerful sense of compassion for others. I witnessed it all my life. His life was built around hard work, honesty, and a love for my mother. My father became a father simply by using the love in his heart.

My uncle, Tom Dunn, was a jack of all trades. There was nothing that man could not do. He could build a house, rebuild a car, bake great cornbread, carve exquisite art, and remain patiently silent as his wife talked on and on.

Tom was a strong, handsome man with deep-set dimples and a shy demeanor. He was one of those fathers who flew under the radar, but the day he flew to heaven, his sons would forever feel an enormous loss. We all would.

What I remember most about Tom was the magical way he would hold a baby. It was as if all the love that lived within his soul spilled into the heart of the child gazing adoringly into his eyes.

This strong man was weakened by pure love. This shy, quiet man was one of the finest fathers I ever knew.

John Alexander Pugh stood 6'2 with dark hair and coal black

eyes. He would stand with his hands on his hips, his pipe in his mouth, and gaze into the morning sunshine as if the new day was just waiting for him to conquer.

He was fierce and correct. He was a man of principle, a man who showed passion, and a man who taught us all to do the right thing.

My Grandfather was respected by all who knew him. He lived by God's laws and faithfully, dutifully served Him.

When he passed away on a warm August day in the summer of 1965, I walked onto the porch of Granddaddy's home. I saw my father standing alone looking toward the lumber mill my grandfather owned.

Tears streamed down his cheeks as he said, "He was the only father I ever knew. I not only was blessed to live my life with his daughter, but he taught me how to live."

My uncle, Paul Walker, was a skillful surgeon. He had one son. His only child lived a life of psychological sadness and pain. Paul did everything he could for Paul, Jr., but nothing worked. His particular skill could not heal the incurable heartache of the illness Paul Jr. bore all his life.

When my uncle retired from his career with the United States Public Health Service, he could have set up a lucrative practice anywhere in the country. He chose the western portion of West Virginia to start a clinic for the most indigent of patients, the coal miners and the people of Appalachia, who until then, had experienced very poor medical care.

He worked for many years saving countless lives, many of those being children. His pain at losing his own child moved him to heal as many children as possible so they could return home to their own grateful fathers.

Great fathers are those who exemplify pure love. The pure love of Uncle Tom building a cradle for a grandchild or helping his son restore a car. The pure love of the granddad who makes sure we get to Sunday School on time to learn about our great heavenly Father. The pure love of the doctor who transforms his own pain into saving the children of other fathers. The pure love of the dad who not only understands his own misfortunes, but teaches his children how to turn tragedy to triumph through pure courage and compassion.

A great father is born of the heart. A father is not great because of money, success, or fame. A great father is the man who measures his own joy and peace by the happiness of his children.

above: Ray Caraway Walker
circa 1934

Tom & Mary Ruth Pugh Dunn
circa 1945

John Alexander Pugh,
maternal grandfather,
circa 1950

The Ten-Year-Old Gift

There are so many things we take for granted in life. The air we breathe, the flowers we pass, the warmth of a home, and even the family beside us.

When we are young we dream of white picket fences surrounding a house filled with a happy family, a smooth road lined with roses, and success.

As we age, we wake up to find reality is a picket fence that always needs a coat of paint, and a potholed road lined with few flowers. Families that have no resemblance to those in the dream, and moments of life that take our breath away. And maybe, the success we envisioned was not what we thought it would be.

However, the one thing that is as close to the dream and to heaven is the miracle of a child. Children are not a dream, but they can fulfill one.

For some, creating a child is difficult. For others, planning to have a baby in January, another in two years happens easily. In my family, for three generations, to be blessed with a child was never easy.

My heart continually goes out to families that struggle with wanting to have children and can't. My feathers get ruffled, when folks that can take it for granted.

My middle daughter, Heather, was married for several years, and had been trying to add to her family for a while. One evening, while I was on vacation at the beach, my phone rang. I took the phone to the balcony and as I looked out at the calming ocean God had created, I was told that He had created another gift for all of us.

How joyous we were! Finally, a child was on its way!

The eight months that followed were not easy due to many complications. Finally, on a warm Sunday evening in June, Avery Elizabeth, came into our world. We knew we were blessed.

All grandparents think their grandchildren are special. I was to learn just how much this one would be over the next ten years.

By the time Avery was in first grade, she had established herself as a good child, an excellent little student, and very sensitive to others' feelings. "Kind," was how she was described, as well as "everyone's friend." She was just sunshine to us all.

Then she became my hero.

At the very beginning of first grade, her mother was diagnosed with cancer. Our world came tumbling down. Whatever life was before; it would never be again.

I hope you never have to explain cancer to a six-year-old. As much as we tried to educate Avery about this disease, it was hard for her to understand until the day her mother came home from the hospital after the first surgery.

I was standing in the kitchen in their Florida home and Avery was in her room. When Heather and her husband came home from the hospital, Heather was weak and frail. Avery came running out to greet her mom. Her broad smile faded as she looked up at the beautiful mom she had known all her life. Suddenly, she understood cancer. She and her mom collapsed on the tile floor in an embrace that brings tears to my eyes as I write this. The bravado that Heather had displayed all along disappeared into the arms of her daughter as they both wept.

Afterwards, Avery became hope. She rallied the family. She made us laugh through the tears. Her life became so paramount in our family that courage and resolve replaced tears. Heather was so inspired by her daughter that she battled through many surgeries, chemo, and radiation. Finally life returned—albeit changed.

Heather became a fighter because of her little girl. Avery's Aunt Amy moved to Florida from her beloved Seattle to be close to her niece and sister. Friends, close and distant, lifted all of us up in prayer. The rest of us just simply thanked the Lord above for every day that followed. We have never again taken for granted the air we breathe.

Avery's maturity during crisis, her understanding of faith, and her enormous capacity for love fills more vases than a thousand roses.

When Avery and I visit, it is our ritual to talk right before sleep in the dark of night. On a recent visit, I was thinking to myself how much I loved this child lying beside me. Suddenly, she reached over me and said, "I love you, Grandma. You are the best Grandma ever! My friends think so too!"

Tears filled my eyes, I hugged her tight, and realized I understood the true meaning of "success." All the years of working hard, every dollar I earned, every coat of fresh paint on that white picket fence was nothing compared to the wonder of this precious ten-year-old.

The Bible says, "Children are a gift from God; they are His reward to you." We should never take for granted a child's love and life. If you are so blessed, a child will warm your home, pick you a flower, and take your breath away.

The Last Layer Of An Angel's Childhood

A week ago, I packed my car with a few tools, my sewing machine, paint brushes, and a piece of art. I drove from Atlanta to Ft. Lauderdale to help redecorate my granddaughter's bedroom.

"Grandma, I want more of a 'beachy look' with pale blue walls," she declared.

I almost quoted my hourly design rate as she rattled off her wishes and hopes. I forgot for a moment she was not a client, but my nearly thirteen-year-old angel whom I love.

As most of you know, my past career was as an Interior Designer. I retired two years ago, but it seems as if my family did not get the notice. They also never pay and are the most difficult of customers.

A designer's family never believes any décor advice you professionally give them. If we charged them, they sure would! It is a standard joke in my clan.

So, it wasn't a surprise when my angel looked at me and said, "But, Grandma, that won't look good!" I laughed and remembered she is just a member of the same clan.

My aha moment came with the first brush stroke of pale blue paint on the wall. I was covering the aqua that had surrounded Avery for over five years of her life. Before that, pale yellow was the color she saw when she first lay in her crib.

When I was an official designer, I would recommend the first rooms to focus on when turning a house into a home are the family room, breakfast and kitchen area.

As an official grandmother, I have changed my mind. If you are a parent of children under eighteen, focus first on their rooms.

The memories we have of our childhood bedrooms are significant. How many of you remember the bedrooms of your childhood? I moved quite a bit through my first eighteen years, but I recall every room which was called mine. When I was a baby, my Uncle Paul gifted me a pencil drawing of two little puppies. That drawing hung in each of my bedrooms, moved with me throughout all the moves of my life, and hangs in my office today.

The last bedroom of my youth was in the house my parents built in LaGrange, Georgia. I drove by the house the last time I was in town. I stopped the car for a bit, gazing at the front corner double windows.

Through those windows, I could see Mama sewing the curtains that fell from the wall canopy above the iron bed. I could see the washstand with the puppy drawing above it, and the stuffed animals that were perched perfectly on top of the wooden canopy. I could see the phone sitting on the built-in desk where I wrote my first story, and I could hear the laughter of my girlfriends when they spent the night.

The room was special because my mother had made it so. Every detail was perfect because she knew it was the last room of my childhood.

The brushstrokes have turned my angel's bedroom into pale blue. The white gauze and linen duvet covers the iron bed. Curtains fall from a white pole with beach themed string lights draped along with them. An old wooden desk sits in the corner with a place for pencils, markers, artist brushes and pens.

Beach signs, a paddle, shells, rope, and burlap have entirely turned the room into the last chapter of my granddaughter's youth. How quickly did those thirteen years go!

It was just yesterday I stood on the ladder turning beige walls to pale yellow as I became downright giddy thinking of the baby who would soon be my grandchild. Wasn't it yesterday when I searched for the right aqua to match the quilt that topped her bed during her elementary days?

I have had the pleasure of being a part of the layers creating the memories she will carry of her childhood home. Her room is where she began her dreams and where her mother and father cradled and comforted her.

It is where we played dolls and whispered secrets in the dark of night. It is where I told her stories about our family that made her laugh. It is where a little girl will become a woman.

"Thank you, Grandma, I love my room!" she yelled as she waved goodbye.

Maybe one far away day, she will drive past the old house of her youth, look through the windows and see me on a ladder, paintbrush in hand, turning walls into a heavenly pale shade of blue for the angel she knew I always loved.

Avery Elizabeth Nystrum, age 13
my granddaughter

The Delightful Legacies They Leave

Everyone has, wants, needs, or misses the crazy and entertaining relatives who bring fun to our lives. These are witty, "never know what they are going to do" sorts who give us laughter, memories, and a happy realization some folks are just a little on the zany side. My family produced an over-abundance of these fun-loving folks.

My mother was quiet and reserved, unlike her sister, Mary Ruth, who never stopped talking long enough to experience quiet. She was four years younger than mom, and even though she is now ninety-four, she still flashes a sparkle of youth in her soul.

When I was a child, I remember believing my aunt was near my age. She loved to laugh, loved to play, and loved to love. Mary was the most beautiful woman I ever knew. Her dark hair and model looks were nothing compared to her kind heart. Priceless Mary was also smart; she married the quietest, most patient man on earth knowing it would allow her to keep talking without interruptions.

I visited her several months ago. She is frail, has dementia, and is a bit quieter now. However, when she saw me approaching, her eyes lit up.

"Mom, do you know who this is?" her son, Mark, asked as we walked toward her.

"Well, that's Lynn!" she exclaimed with a broad smile illuminating her face.

We walked back to her room where family pictures adorned the dresser and photo albums were stacked neatly on a bookshelf. We started leafing through the pages and snickered as we recalled the folks and events depicted in the old pictures.

Dementia had not erased Mary's playfulness. She will not remember I visited her, but I will never forget this happy, spirited, warm ray of sunshine who played an essential role in my life.

My friend, Deborah, tells tales about her mother's sister and her Aunt Teeny. In the 1960s, South Carolina probably was too small to hold the likes of Teeny when she decided to go to beauty school at age forty, along with two of her daughters. Later, when anyone wanted to visit Teeny, you did so at the beauty shop except on Mondays when they closed. Many Monday afternoons Teeny would pick up her sister and the kids after school and travel to Charlotte in her Ford Woody station wagon.

Every trip was an adventure, including getting lost, getting stopped for speeding and making detours to discount stores for Teeny's cigarettes. Yes, Teeny smoked, bleached her dark hair blond, sang off-color songs, always had an entourage, spoke her mind, water skied, rode horses, bowled, played cards, and any other game she could talk someone into playing.

However, just like my Aunt Mary Ruth, Teeny was a fantastic cook, loved and was loved by all children, and could make each person in her life feel special.

Aunt Teeny was irreverent, yet Deborah states, "I never heard her judge another person. She lived her faith, and until the day she died, never lost her zeal for life. She was everyone's favorite aunt even if they weren't related!"

Twenty years ago, when my eldest nephew was two, the family gathered for a wedding in Tennessee. We were staying in a hotel where one morning I was racing my toddler nephew down the halls. Everyone came out of their rooms and started laughing at the two of us.

My daughter Amy (bless her heart) pointed at me and asked, "Alex, do you know her actual name?" Seeing the puzzled look in his eyes, she continued, "Her real name is Crazy Aunt Lynn!"

"Cwazy Aunt Wynn?" he repeated.

From that day forward, I had a new name. If I were doing something wacky, Alex would say, "Cwazy Aunt Wynn, you are going to get in weal twouble!"

"Of course, Alex I am going to be in "real trouble" and so are you!" Then we would laugh and keep on getting into mischief.

Alex is now in pre-med, and no longer gets into "twouble." Austin, his brother, is also in college and they both still call me my "real name." I also have three other nieces and nephews all under the age of six.

Samantha, my six-year-old niece, recently overheard a conversation between her grandmother and her parents regarding my writing.

"Wait, who are you talking about?" she inquired.

"Aunt Lynn," they responded.

Looking confused, Samantha said, "You mean Crazy Aunt Lynn?!"

I have become the goofy, zany, irreverent, trouble-making aunt I always aspired to be. I hope to join the club of those never forgotten, story-laden folks who might bring a smile to a face one day just like Mary Ruth and Teeny do to the nieces who live in their shadows.

How blessed we are to know those who bring sparkle to our lives and leave a legacy of abundant delight.

Sarah Elizabeth Holley
"Teeny"
circa 1990

Mary Ruth Pugh Dunn
circa 1944

Faith

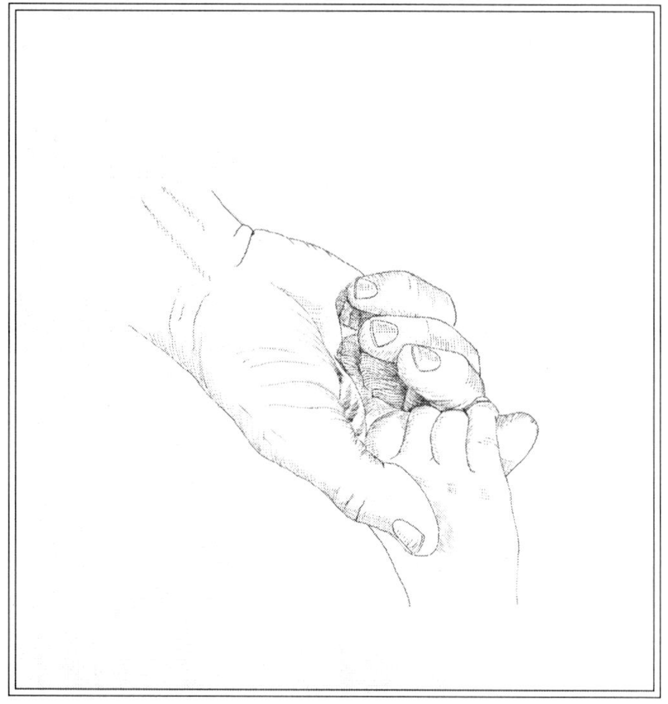

The Lord often speaks to people in ways each of his children understands. For some He whispers, for some He yells, for others He draws pictures. He talks to me using all the tools He has.

I have always felt the presence of the Lord beside me. I am closer to Him when I write. When I stare at a blank page wondering how I will find words to fill it, He uses my hands to tap the keys.

God is my greatest gift, my best friend, the author of my soul and the peace in my world.

I would have never made it through life without Him nor would I have wanted to.

"Love God, Love People"

It was early spring in Georgia. The azaleas were blooming in glorious shades of pinks and corals. The dogwoods were awash in white blossoms, and the hardwood trees were born anew into living green.

My three children were all under the age of seven, and it was my day off. Every so often when they were small, I would gather a quilt and a basket to enjoy a picnic.

The sky was void of clouds, and the sun was starting to warm the chilly day. Our picnic spot was in a beautiful park with a lake surrounded by manicured perfection. Swans and ducks swam as children ran and played. One willow tree hung over the water's edge as the wind gently swayed its branches. Squirrels scampered, and birds flew. It was a Monet masterpiece moment on that early April day in the Georgia sunshine.

When we sat down to eat our little sandwiches, I held my son in my lap as the girls giggled trying to keep their napkins from blowing away.

"Kids, what is the most beautiful sight in the park today?" I questioned.

Amy, the oldest, said, "The white swan, Mama!"

I responded, "No, not to me."

"I know, I know!!!" shouted Heather. "It's the flowers!"

"No, not to me." I repeated.

"The twee, the twee!" Corey pointed to the weeping willow that fascinated him.

"No, son, not to me," I whispered as he cuddled in my arms.

"What is it, Mama?" the girls shouted.

"Try to remember these words. You see, to me, the most

beautiful sight in this park is the people. God made these gorgeous trees, flowers, and animals, but His park was not complete until His final creation. And, that was all of us.

"You, my children, are the most beautiful sight I see in the park."

The memory of that day has stayed deep in my heart for forty years. If I close my eyes, I can still see those adorable faces with the April breeze blowing their wispy blond hair just as it swept the wispy branches of the willow tree.

I have always loved people. From the time I was a toddler, my mother said I was never afraid to meet a stranger. People, to me, were fascinating and intriguing. I would talk to anyone and still do. Nothing much has changed.

Now, I have met some folks along my life journey that I wouldn't care to go to dinner with, but very few. And, some people have taken an evil route in life, and I hope never to meet them. However, I often wonder why they became so evil? What made them turn from small curious children into monsters? Did anyone hold them in their lap and whisper love to them?

I experienced a bit of bullying at a young age. I had an extraordinary reaction to it. I cried and prayed, but I never felt revenge or hate. As I grew older and found myself hurt by a loved one or two, I decided that I would just keep caring for these special folks even though they were gone. I know what you're thinking; and, yes, I am kind of weird.

God made all of us for a reason. He loves every single person including the weird ones like me. To every person on earth, He gave a simple rule: "Love me, and love others as I love you." Boy, if we could all follow that simple rule, the world would be fixed. Right? We are not perfect and don't follow the rules well, but even in our imperfection, we find His abiding love. I do know that hate and resentment get us nowhere.

Sometimes when we love deeply and it is not returned, we hurt. However, the only thing that can cure the sting of having loved is to love again. When I chose to love the bully and the folks who caused my heart to break, I decided to give them to God. Doing so seemed to take away my pain and give me the two gifts that only love can bring: compassion and forgiveness.

After all these years, that bully is now my buddy. The friends I'm sure I've disappointed at times are still my friends. I keep old loves in my heart, and my children are still the most beautiful sight in the park.

My scarred heart is well, and my soul is at peace because I choose to love God and His people.

Climbing The Rock Mountain

The time between a cancer diagnosis and starting treatment is gut-wrenching, shocking, scary, and heartbreaking. The first thought is, "This can't be happening!" and the second is, "Will I make it?"

When my daughter was diagnosed with cancer in 2011, it was such a thunderbolt I thought there was some cosmic mistake. How could a 37-year-old, tiny, mother of one with no family history be diagnosed with breast cancer? Yes, this is wrong.

However, within 24 hours our world, as we knew it as a family, was tossed aside like a twig in a wind storm. The diagnosis was correct and pleading with God began.

Every day for weeks all I did was beg. I would take a daily walk down the Florida streets where Heather lived and just repeat, "Please, please, God, please."

Those days became cast in granite as the worst days of our family's collective lives. Those days of not knowing and having to learn. Those days of screaming, crying, and more begging. Those days of complications, deciding treatment courses, more doctors, and more hand-holding.

The day that you must tell a six-year-old that her world is no longer pain-free. Those days you must watch the heartache unfold before your eyes as the reality of living and losing becomes almost unbearable.

I can't tell you exactly when I had the dream, but it was one of those restless, exhausted nights followed by one of those days. The dream began with my struggle to climb up a rocky mountain. Each boulder was sharp and angled with different cuts and jagged edges. I started to climb, desperately knowing I had to reach the apex. I would turn a ridge and scrape my knees and cut my hands, but, determined, I kept lifting myself toward the top. Everything was gray—the sky, the rocks, the air. There was no sun, no rain, no clouds of white, no sign of life.

Then I eyed the top of the mountain. I stopped on a large rock surface and was on my knees getting ready to climb again when I knew I could go no further.

There He was. A towering figure dressed in gray looking upward toward the heavens of doom above him. He seemed to be the actual crest of the mountain as if he carved himself into the stone.

I did not want Him to be real. In his arms was a deceased woman. Her arms dangled from her side, and her hair was falling toward the ground in damp gray strings. He held onto my lifeless daughter and looked above as a tear ran down his cheek. I wanted to scream, yet, no sound came from my mouth.

I couldn't retrieve her from the man. I couldn't plead for her to come alive. All I could do was look to the gray God above me as he lifted her up. Then His eyes met mine.

Not a word was spoken between us, but I knew her soul was in His hands. She belonged to Him. There was nothing I could do. I started to climb back down into the green of the world below without her, and that is when I woke up.

Perspiration soaked my nightgown. Tears were falling down my cheeks, and I tried not to sob openly. I was shaking so violently that I thought I would wake my granddaughter lying beside me.

The next morning the dream haunted me as I drank my coffee. With a certainty I can't explain, I knew what it all meant and what God expected from me.

Courageously, I was to ask people to pray. I was to write about our experiences and share them. I was not to beg God but beg others for prayer. I began calling on people I had not conversed with in years and emailing churches that I never visited.

I reached out to my old high school class, and they spread

their prayers across the country along with my clients, my friends, and my family.

There was no shame in asking everyone for prayers. When my daughter wanted privacy, I told her I usually would do whatever she asked, but not this time. It was incredibly difficult not to honor her wishes. However, I knew God knew it would be.

The prayers spread and with them, hope and courage grew.

One morning while alone, it dawned on me what the rest of the dream meant. I realized that even though I bore this daughter, she was not mine. She had always belonged to God, her father.

All our children are gifts from God. He loans them to us to love, raise, and teach. Not all children are born in perfect health, and many will not live to adulthood, but they are still His gifts. To trust God to know what He is doing with your child is faith beyond going to church.

The dream of climbing the rock mountain taught me that no matter what happened, I had to trust God.

I learned that I couldn't control life, disease, or death. The only thing I could manage was my faith and obedience to God.

Heather's cancer journey began six years ago, and she still thrives in the green below the mountain. I never stopped writing and sharing. I learned that there is only one person that could love my child more than her mother. He is the Father who wept on top of a rock mountain.

A Stone's Throw To "Forgiveness"

How many people do you know who carry a grudge? How many times when someone dies, have you heard someone close to them say, "I wish I had told them...?"

My father was a gregarious, talkative person. Folks say we are alike. I received plenty of good advice from Dad throughout my life. Some of his sage wisdom I followed and some I didn't. Usually, he was right, I was wrong, and he never had a problem saying, "I told you so."

On a cold, sunny, November day years ago, my father left this earth from a hospital room. He had been there four days, and at 85, was ready for his heavenly home. He had no fear whatsoever. I admired that.

As his eyes were closing, I walked over to him, took his hand and whispered, "Thank you, Dad, for being my father, for taking loving care of all of us. You did a great job!" A tear rolled down his cheek, and without opening his eyes, he replied, "I am sorry."

Stunned, I responded, "For what?"

"I gave you some bad advice years ago, and you followed it. It was the wrong thing for you to do because it hurt your life." At that point, his tears started to flow. I never knew until that moment he had carried that burden for thirty years.

"Dad, my life became what it was supposed to be. You have nothing to be sorry for at all." He opened his eyes, looked into mine, and said, "Forgive me." I held his hand tighter, and whispered, "I forgave all long ago."

Those were our last words uttered before he walked into an angel's arms.

Six years later, my mother was in her final days. Mom was a quiet person. I loved her dearly, but we were opposites. I tell everybody way too much about everything. Mom never told anyone way too much about anything.

Near the end of her life, she confided that someone had hurt her seventy years prior. Near death, she still was holding on to that little burden of hurt.

Mom lost her first child four days after giving birth. She never discussed it until she told me one day right before her death, "I want to go to heaven to see my baby girl." I never knew her sorrow.

People hang on to hurt, bitterness, sorrow, revenge, and a host of other troubling emotions because they willfully will not speak about them. Is that false pride or being scared to share; or has the pain become a comfortable shadow they can't walk away from?

Sometimes you just have to take all that sorrow, hurt, revenge and bitterness to the river.

Years ago I was hurt badly. I never thought of myself as a revengeful person. I have many faults, but I usually don't hold grudges; except then I sure did. I couldn't sleep, I couldn't think of anything but the pain the other person caused. I had never felt that kind of hate before. I was miserable.

Then I went down to the river near my home. The Chattahoochee flows rapidly between boulders and rocks. It is a place where people love to sit in the summer and watch the water swirl around them.

However, this was winter, and no one was there. The solitude embraced me and the rushing water's roar was enough to drown the demon voices in my mind.

"God, you say revenge is yours. So take it from me. I loathe the hate within me. I am ashamed I can't forgive; I am miserable. Please help me."

I prayed those words as earnestly as I could. I picked up a

large rock and said aloud, "Here it is, this stone of burden, you can have it, God, it's yours." I threw the stone into the river as far as I could.

The minute I saw it disappear into the swift current was the minute the pain was gone. I slept soundly that night. God forgave me for hating, and I forgave the person who hurt me. It was the fastest response I ever received from a prayer in my life.

There are families everywhere whose members don't speak to each other. They are stuck, can't forgive, can't forget. People are walking around with so many internal grudges they have forgotten how to enjoy much of anything.

We spend valuable time being afraid of what people think. We think winning with stubbornness is stronger than losing ourselves in the freedom of forgiveness.

To say, "I am sorry," or "I forgive you," takes courage. Just three little words wash away all the bad ones. Would you rather carry a heavy burden, or would you just as soon let God have it to throw in the swift water?

Another man was on His way to heaven like my father. He had been beaten, persecuted, and betrayed. Before He closed His eyes, He looked down from His cross and said, "Forgive them for they know not what they do."

If He could forgive, should we not do the same? Is it time to go down to the river?

Angels Among The Blackberries

Just south of Atlanta in McDonough, Georgia is a treasure called Southern Belle Farms. Owned by the Carter Family, this 330-acre farm is open to the public in the summer so folks can pick beautiful and bountiful fruits.

When the green of summer turns to the browns and golds of fall, the farm turns to corn mazes, hayrides, campfires and pumpkin patches which attract hordes of families and yellow buses filled with school children.

Several years ago, when my granddaughter Avery came for her regular summer visit, my friend Deborah and I took her toddler grandson, Whit, and Avery down to pick blackberries. We decided it was time to teach these city kids a bit about farm life.

Whit ate more blackberries than he picked and was stained red from head to toe. Avery, who was then eight, just loved it all.

Every summer since, we gather the two of them to visit the rolling hills, pet the animals and have a picnic in the summer sun. We look forward to trading the skyscrapers of the city for the tall silos beside the red roof barns.

The Carter family has owned Southern Belle Farms since 1938. It was a dairy farm until the economy changed and the Carters started growing berries. Row after row of beautiful fresh berries pulled in customers with cash and the farm survived.

When we visited this year, the blackberries, strawberries and peaches ripened at the same time. Deborah and I were dreaming of pies and cobblers while Whit was still eating blackberries by the dozen.

We stayed longer than other times and went to visit Belle, the big jersey cow and also the new "Country Market" erected since the previous June.

The market was quite impressive with its rocking chair-filled porch and stocked shelves of ripe peaches and preserves. Beams of wood and beams on smiling faces filled the store.

As impressive as it was and as enjoyable as it all is, there is a story or two which makes you think not only about how Mother Nature works, but also about how a bountiful God controls her.

Jake Carter is a young man who took over the day-to-day operation of the farm after graduating from the University of Georgia several years ago. He's a Christian man who looks to God for guidance as he takes on this daily responsibility.

Crops only produce what God and mother nature allow. As we all know, you can have an abundance of berries or none depending on how the raindrops fall.

In June 2009 the blackberries were growing wonderfully well when suddenly they became unhealthy. Not understanding the cause, Jake walked among the rows, and as he watched them wither, he prayed.

He noticed a bit of trash on the ground. As he walked toward the shiny object, he realized it was a silver mylar balloon that had landed in the middle of a row.

When he retrieved it, he saw a laminated note attached with a ribbon. After reading it, he learned the balloon traveled from Talladega, Alabama to McDonough, Georgia, finally landing in the blackberry row with this message from the book of Jeremiah in the Bible:

"For I know the plans I have for you," declares the Lord, "Plans to prosper you, plans to give you hope and a future."

For years, Jake had pondered the thought of extending the operation to include a store. Expanding the farm was such a difficult financial decision he had wrestled with for so long that he finally gave himself a timeline: June 2015.

Finally, the day came when he and his family were to have a meeting with a contractor at 9:30 am. He awoke that morning and prayed about the decision, still unsure and wavering.

It had been a busy, anxious morning. About fifteen minutes before the meeting, Jake decided to take the little farm buggy around to check on the produce.

When he neared the blackberries, a young woman ran out from one of the berry rows.

"Can you help me?" She looked alarmed. "I am here with my Mom, and she is not well!"

Jake jumped off the buggy and ran to the elderly woman. The woman was stricken with rheumatoid arthritis and indeed was not doing well. Jake was getting ready to lift her to his buggy when she did a most unusual thing.

Jake Carter's grandmother had suffered from rheumatoid arthritis. She had passed away several years before, but this woman instantly reminded him of his beloved grandmother. As he was leaning over to assist her, the woman looked into his eyes and touched his heart with her crippled hand.

"I will pray for you to prosper. God is with you, and He has plans for you."

Chills ran over Jake, and he realized as she continued to speak the more she sounded as if she was indeed his departed grandmother.

He delivered the women safely to their car, but the encounter made him a bit late for the meeting with the contractor. He never saw or heard from the mother and daughter again.

Jake Carter went on to build the market with not an ounce of fear in his heart.

I had thought many times about interviewing Jake to write a story Southern Belle Farms, but never got around to call. One Thursday morning as I walked out of the gym, I prayed about my article due that week. A title for an article about the farms came to me out of the blue: Angels Among the Blackberries.

I immediately called Jake. After an introduction, we chatted. It seems that Jake had asked God on this same beautiful July day to use his farm for the glory of God.

You see God works in beautiful, crazy, ways. Ways we cannot understand, ways we cannot see, ways to make us have better lives and make us better believers. God sees potential and prosperity in all of his children if we only listen to His whispers and believe that He can also send angels to walk among the blackberries.

The Pope And Five Protestants

It was right before Christmas in 2011, when my two daughters and I were sitting at a breakfast table looking as if the world had ended. My middle daughter, 38-year-old Heather, was fighting effects from the last rounds of chemotherapy. Her sister had flown in from Seattle to help.

Avery, Heather's daughter, was in school that particular morning when the three of us were left staring into coffee mugs, and silence filled the air. Heather was leaning on her arm as if her head couldn't hold itself up. Her pale face was still beautiful while the scarf she wore around her head was neatly tied and quite pretty.

Amy sipped her coffee while her dark eyes seemed troubled and scared.

"You know what?!" My voice split the deafening silence.

Heather's head raised off her arm. Amy's eyes widened.

"If we make it through this whole mess intact, I am taking us to Italy!"

It had always been a dream to take my family to Europe. I had been saving points on my credit card for years. I wasn't even sure how many I had accumulated but knew it was impressive. Those points were my own little savings plan.

My husband, David, and I, along with his two girls and my son, had been to Italy in 2005. Avery was a newborn and couldn't go, so I always hoped one day I would be able to take my girls. I fell in love with Italy. When you have an Italian name like Gendusa, you feel as if you belong.

The three of us refilled our coffee cups as we started to dream. Amy and Heather weren't sure the trip would ever take place, but the silence was briefly interrupted, and I saw a tiny spark in Heather's eyes.

Well, to make a very long story short, five people boarded a plane bound for Rome on a sunny day in March 2013. Heather and her husband Mike, Avery, Amy, and myself. David could not go because of business, but we did have his blessing.

We chose March because of spring break for Avery. March would also find Italy less crowded and not as hot.

We were to start in Rome, then to Tuscany, then off to the Amalfi Coast. I booked the trip one year in advance and dared cancer to mess with me. There was something within me that pushed and pushed until we made a spark become fire. We all planned that trip down to the last detail. Nothing was going to stop us!

Then Pope Benedict resigned. The Papal Conclave would be held in Rome on the Monday following the very weekend we were to tour the Vatican. We were to meet our guide, Maria, in St. Peter's square on Saturday morning, March 9, 2013, at 8 a.m.

To say the world descended on Rome is an understatement. People were everywhere.

I had said many times throughout my daughter's yearlong battle with cancer, my faith went to a new level. I gave God my daughter, trusting Him and His will. Now, her scarves were in a drawer somewhere, her eyes always sparkled, and life was returning to some normalcy.

St. Peters square is awe-inspiring. It's the place where huge crowds gather to catch a glimpse of the Pope and to be blessed. The Obelisk, in the center, is supposedly the site where Romans crucified the apostle Peter. When you gaze at the Obelisk, realizing where you are, it is a "chills" moment.

We met Maria, and she was lovely. She took a particular interest in telling Avery all which she was about to see in a way only an eight-year-old can understand. The crowds had not yet arrived, so the square was reasonably empty.

Since I had visited the Vatican on my prior trip, I stepped

away from the family and turned to look at the scene around us. The Basilica was behind me, and the Catholic Cardinals who assembled from around the world were all in the Vatican apartments to my left. The newly erected media scaffolding stood around the perimeter of the square. The news media had not yet arrived; birds flew in circles above us, and workers were putting the smoke stack on the Sistine Chapel.

While I was standing in the midst of this very Holy place, I saw a lone figure in the far left corner of the square walking from outside the Vatican into the square.

The only reason I would notice this man in the distance was the scarlet red of his scarf at the waist of his vestment and on his Biretta adorning the top of his head.

My first thought, *Is that a Cardinal and if so what is he doing out here?* was followed by *Surely it is only someone dressed to resemble one.*

My eyes fixated on him as he moved closer and closer. He cut a diagonal path across the square as if aiming right at this little cluster of a family with a guide named Maria.

We are a family of Protestants, but I knew something was awry for this Cardinal to be doing what he was doing. The closer he came, the more Maria's eyes widened. She, too, stopped talking.

I thought surely he would go around us, but no, he walked between us. I touched the sleeve of his Simar, noticed his ring, and then he bowed his head to us. He smiled and he and I both conversed, but neither of us understood the other due to language barriers.

I watched him stroll away, noticing his hands, the back of his head, his glasses, his gait and then turned to Maria.

"Is that normal?" I questioned.

"No," she replied. "Maybe this Cardinal will be our new Papa!"

My favorite verse in the Bible is a simple one. Many years ago while I was going through a fierce struggle, I prayed earnestly. My Bible fell on the floor and opened to this red-letter quote, "Daughter your faith has made you well."

In all of our struggles in life, it is our faith that can heal us. Not only from sickness, but within our hearts and souls. Faith is a brace for our lives. It provides us the strength to go through our trials and tribulations. Without faith, there are no lasting sparkles of hope.

Jorge Mario Bergoglio confirmed to five touring Protestants, that because they had faith, they were blessed by God through a man whose name would change forever in three short days to..."Pope Francis."

The Joy Of Seeing Footprints

When I was a little girl, every time I saw a puddle I would walk through it and then watch my footprints form on the dry part of the pavement. The other day was no exception. I just can't resist.

There are some things we never outgrow. When I was young, watching the footprints form was just a fun thing to do. Now when I see the outline of my feet, a sincere appreciation fills my soul.

Mary Stevenson wrote a beautiful poem in 1936 called, "Footprints in the Sand." There is valuable wisdom is in her words.

In the early 1980's a friend cross-stitched the poem, framed it, and gave it to me as a gift because she knew how much I loved it. It hangs in my hall, and I visit it often to read the words, that today, I truly understand.

There is not a person on earth who hasn't experienced moments that stop our hearts, or hours that were unbearable. Phone calls that brought devastating news and disbelief. How did we survive?

When we were both just fifteen, I watched my good friend go through the loss of her mother. I remember thinking, "If I were her, I couldn't stand it! I would surely die!" But she was somehow standing strong. "How?"

"I think the Lord is helping me," she said when I asked her.

As I journeyed further into life, I experienced a tough time in my twenties. I remember saying, "I can't survive this!" My strength was gone, life was entirely on the brink, and I could not see tomorrow at all.

Well, I am writing you today! "How?"

I have watched sadness unfold all around me. I have witnessed friends who have suffered a myriad of tragedies including children's deaths or devastating illnesses. These same friends who have experienced profound, deep heartaches are today smiling, giving, and moving onward. Difficult? Yes, of course, but, "How?"

People ask me many times, "How did you survive some of the things you went through?" When they do, I think of my friend, Kathy, and repeat her words. "I think the good Lord helped me."

Many folks have a hard time understanding the fantastic gifts that God gives us to survive in this life. The gift of faith is just one of them. For me, it is the most important of all.

When terrible misfortunes come our way, a lot of people ask, "Why did God allow this to happen?" I understand. I think since we don't yet live in paradise, terrible things are going to continue to happen. None of us is immune to tragedy and sorrow.

I don't blame God for the heartache life hands me. I just learned to take His hand. I feel God cries when I do, just like any good father would.

Faith gives us the ability to reach up for help and honestly believe that we will one day see those whom we mourn, those who have suffered unbelievable heartache, alive and well in a place that is paradise.

I know I sound right "preachy" here, but having lived a while, I know it is just the gospel truth.

When I glance back upon my life, I realize that the only way I passed through tough times was because God picked me up and carried me down the road. There is no way I could have done it on my own.

There are two categories you can drop into when tragedy strikes. You can fall into resentment, anger, or into a spiritual abyss. Or, you can fall into the arms of God and let him carry you when you can't walk. When you allow God to share your tragedy, your strength will rise, your faith will sustain you, and it is incredible how that God-given courage carries forward.

Kathy's strength did. So many have picked up grief and moved it to help others. They have replaced tears with smiles, and hopelessness with faith. When they do, God just shines right through them.

"Lord, you said that once I decided to follow you, you'd walk with me all the way. But I have noticed that during the most troublesome times in my life there is only one set of footprints.

"I don't understand why when I needed you most you would leave me."

The Lord replied:

"My precious child, I love you, and I would never leave you.

"During your times of trial and suffering, when you only saw one set of footprints, it was then that I carried you."

—*Mary Stevenson, 1936*

Yes, I still walk through puddles today. I look back at my footprints and realize I always see, through faith, four.

A Sign At Grandpa's On A Summer Sunday

From the time I was two until I was twenty-two, I visited my grandmother for two weeks at the beginning of every summer. I hope you remember the story as to why I called her "Grandpa" instead of Grandma or Nana or any other suitable "grand" names. However, in case you did not read the original explanation, this will aid you.

Grandpa's first-born grandson, my brother, was living in the same town as five generations of grandmothers on both sides of his family and only one living grandfather. As a three-year-old boy, it was mighty confusing when he yelled "Grandma," and six grandmothers ran to him.

He stubbornly began calling his favorite of the grandmother bunch "Grandpa," and no one could make him stop. She was Grandpa to every child who knew her for the rest of her 97 years.

My Aunt Mary and her boys were coming to visit on the first Sunday I arrived at Grandpa's house in my 10th year. We were all planning to go swimming that afternoon. I went down the hall to get the swimsuit out of my luggage only to find my mother had not packed one.

When I realized the horror of such a misdeed, a sure-fire ten-year-old hissy fit lit up the house.

"Lord, what's the matter, child?" Grandpa yelled as she ran toward the bedroom.

"Mama didn't pack my swimsuit!" I blubbered, blabbered, and blurted out in a yell.

"Lord, I thought the house was on fire!" Grandpa said, relieved when she saw the only thing blazing was my face.

Once she calmed me, we started walking back toward the kitchen. She was going to call Aunt Mary to see what they could do about finding me a suit. I'll remind you back in those days the only thing open on Sunday was the church and they didn't sell swim attire.

As Grandpa was dialing Mary, I noticed an old sign hanging amid some family pictures on the hall wall. The plaque made of cardboard had no frame, but a hole was punched in the top to let it hang from a nail. It's white stenciled letters read, "I KNOW THE LORD WILL MAKE A WAY FOR ME."

"Lynn, I called your Aunt Mary, and she is going to bring you one of her old swimsuits. I know it'll be too big but, shoot, we can pin that suit up, and it'll be just fine!" Grandpa merrily stated.

"I know," I assuredly replied.

"Why are you now so sure it will all work out?" Grandpa looked puzzled over my new calm demeanor.

"The sign said it would." I pointed down the hall to the faded little sign hanging on a penny nail. "The Lord told me he would make it happen!"

I swam in the lake that day with my cousins in a suit clinched and pinned together with a myriad of different sized safety pins. The "way too big" suit fell off a couple of times in the water, but I knew the Lord had made a way for me to swim, so I didn't complain.

After Grandpa passed away thirty-seven years later, one of the items she left me was the old sign that hung in her hall. Of course, it has no monetary value but is now proudly displayed above my desk and is priceless.

Sixty summers have passed since I wore Aunt Mary's old black swimsuit. I'll bet I have needed to be reminded sixty thousand times through the years to believe in the words on the sign.

How many times have I thought I wouldn't make it through

a tragedy or a loss? How many moments have I wailed, screamed, and pitched a 10-year-old hissy fit as an adult because I couldn't find my way? How many halls have I paced wondering what to do?

How many times have I worried and fretted over uncontrollable events? How often have I tried to carry the load on my shoulders only to find it too heavy to bear?

Today, I intended to write my weekly column. I started writing three stories and threw them in the trash. A little panic and worry began to wrinkle my brow when I thought I could be experiencing my first case of writer's block.

My Bible was sitting on the edge of my desk. I randomly opened it to see if the Lord's words would spark a few words of my own.

In red letters, "Daughter, your faith has healed you. Go in peace."

At the same time, I noticed the little sign slightly hidden behind my computer screen. I immediately recalled Grandpa telling the story many times about the little girl who visited on a Sunday and had enough faith to believe the words, "I KNOW THE LORD WILL MAKE A WAY FOR ME."

I know He always has, and He always will.

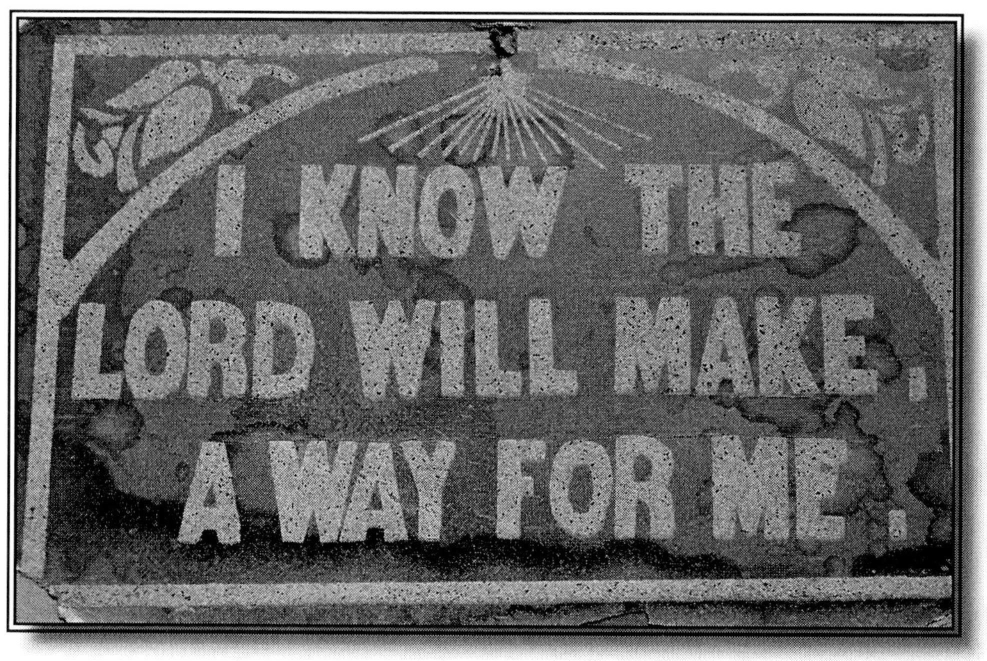
I KNOW THE
LORD WILL MAKE,
A WAY FOR ME.

Roots

RAY WALKER
ELIZABETH PUGH
4/9/1939
JOHN & NANNIE PUGH
MOLLIE & JOHN SPARKS
ROBERT & ROSE WALKER
LOURAY & JAMES WALKER

When we investigate the past to research our heritage, we find more than where we are from; we discover who we are as people.

We acquaint ourselves with those who endured hardships and peril so we may enjoy the richness of today. Those who crossed oceans, those who fought in revolutions, and those who worked hard to ensure future generations would have opportunities.

I have met my ancestors not only with my eyes, but also with my heart. Their bravery is inspiring, their spirits continue to soar, and I am eternally grateful we share the branches of an extraordinary and mighty tree.

The Unsinkable Mollie Sparks

Mollie Randolph was born amid the hardwood trees in Putnam County, Tennessee on December 5, 1876. Her family came to America in 1669 and would call Monterey, Tennessee home for generations.

Mollie's academic education lasted for two years. Like others in that era, all family members worked to put food on the table. The luxury of going to school was just a dream.

She married John Thomas Sparks in 1894. On December 15, 1907, two weeks before her last child was born, her husband tragically died in a sawmill accident. Mollie was left to care for five small children and would eventually raise two granddaughters.

Our history reveals some very famous heroines. Some have walked beside us, and we may never have known it. These outstanding, as well as unsung heroes, are determined by heroic acts that take extreme courage and strength.

Mollie Sparks was a giant among heroines. She stood erect at 4 feet 10 inches tall and weighed a mere 88 pounds her entire adult life. However, she was able to carry the weight of her world on her tiny frame.

After her husband died, she was left indigent. The family lived in a small wooden house with a large garden. No indoor plumbing, no car, no electricity, and no one to assist her with the enormous task of providing for her young family.

Mollie rolled up her sleeves and, from then on, never sat down. She collected laundry around town to wash and iron for folks. The water came from her well, the washing machine was her hands on a washboard, and her iron heated on a wood burning stove.

During the evening after the rest of her daily work ended, she quilted quilts to keep her children warm. Each stitch by her slender, nimble fingers created beautiful, intricate patterns that would be handed down to families she would never meet.

Mollie's hair grew past her waist; she rolled it into a tight bun at the nape of her neck to keep it out of the way. She had a dress she wore every Sunday to church, clasped at the collar with a broach that, I am sure, was a luxury.

She tithed all she could on those Sundays and gave away food to those needier than she. She obeyed the principles of her faith her entire life.

Her children grew into beautiful, sweet caring people, none of them afraid to work and help. She raised them to be kind, reliable, good people. They asked for nothing and never complained.

Her oldest son survived World War I and became a fireman and was burned severely in an explosion. She nursed him back to health but her beautiful boy carried scars for the rest of his life.

Another son died at the age of 38, leaving her to raise his two children. They became nurses and gave all the credit of their living to the life of Mollie Sparks.

Each of her three daughters lived long and productive lives that left an indelible mark on the souls of many.

Mollie lived to be 94 years old. She endured some of her children, grandchildren, and great-grandchildren serving our country in five wars.

She accepted indoor plumbing in her 70s because her son-in-law insisted on building a bathroom for her. She planted a garden every year, and she always cooked her food on the same wood burning stove. She was stubborn, willful, and could rule a clan with an iron fist. You didn't mess with the likes of Mollie Sparks.

She never felt life owed her anything other than what she produced. Mollie worked for all that she had and then gave all she had left to the people who were blessed to know this heroine.

Her belief that kindness, discipline, and faith in God would get you through all things in life was a testimony to a life well-lived. Not lived with an abundance of material items but certainly with an abundant heart.

I often wonder what she would think of this world today?

A world where people complain if the waiter is not getting to them fast enough. A society that has grown less thankful as the years pass. A world where some people believe they are owed something just because they are alive. A world where some applaud vitriol, crave entertainment and teach their children by words instead of actions.

L to R: Nannie Sparks Pugh (Grandpa), Mollie Sparks (great grandmother) Lucille Sparks Pugh, Florida Sparks Johnson, and Casto Sparks in back circa 1950s

I think she would probably get a switch and set us all straight.

Mollie Sparks taught me a lot about life. In my darkest hours when life felt unbearable, I would remember this woman's daily life, and then my problems became very, very small. I could survive anything because her courage and fortitude were inspiring.

My great-grandmother, Mollie Sparks, was unsinkable, undeterred and undeniably great.

Sometimes God creates a heritage to help us find strength from those who walked before us. Sometimes we need to look backward to see that courage, thankfulness, and faith are necessary to travel forward.

The Whispers Of Mollie

Two months ago, I wrote an article titled, "The Unsinkable Mollie Sparks," about my great-grandmother, a diminutive woman with a firm resolve who resided in her small town on top of the Cumberland Plateau in Tennessee from 1876 to 1970.

My widowed great-grandmother was the most financially needy woman in my family that I ever knew. I found her will to survive enormous and heroic. I am in awe of the children she raised. My grandmother, Aunt Lucille, Aunt Florida, Uncle Casto and the rest were just the finest, funniest, people I have ever known. All of them were full of faith, values, and joy. I loved them immensely.

At the beginning of the first story about the unsinkable Mollie, I wanted to include her exact birthday. I couldn't find it, so I decided I would sign up on Ancestry.com to see if by chance she was in a computer somewhere. Logically I knew I didn't need the exact date, but something was pushing me.

Once I entered her info, her picture flashed on the screen. A tear formed in my eye, and suddenly Mollie was sitting beside me. I wrote the story and felt her presence the entire time. However, her story didn't end there.

After I met my deadline for the paper, I went back to the computer to look at her photo again. Her face haunted me as if she were trying to tell me something. I learned how to navigate the ancestry website which sent me further back into her life. I knew who her mother was but knew little about her father, James Robert Randolph. Apparently, no one else did either.

The family history just stopped with him.

I become obsessed with trying to solve the mystery of Mollie's father—my great, great grandfather. After over 100 hours traveling through time with Mollie in the back seat, and James in front pointing me in the right direction, we reached our destination.

Along the way, I met family members I never knew. I had to travel through records I could barely read and blogs from people on similar journeys. I began to understand my complicated heritage and the joy of navigating through each generation on this uncharted path.

We hit a speed bump on the road when I could not locate a record for James' father. His mother never married. Shocked, I kept thinking that couldn't be right! Sadly, it was. James had an older brother as well, who had moved to Texas and changed his name. His mother finally married later in life, left Tennessee and died in Arkansas.

I can't imagine the hardship of being the child of a single unmarried mother in a small town in the 1800s where gossip spreads like poison ivy. However, James stayed in Tennessee, kept his name, and held his head high.

James lived an impoverished life but left a legacy of richness. His courage was passed down through his children and grandchildren. Those whom he bore with his wife, Nancy, gave more value to the lives that followed than all the money in the world could have.

Our road ended in Virginia where we discovered James' heritage in America began with Henry Randolph. Henry came to American in the mid 1600s. Henry, along with his nephew William, was instrumental in the establishment of Colonial Virginia. They lived in Plantations along the James River and were considered one of the wealthiest and most influential families in America. President Thomas Jefferson's mother was Jane Randolph Jefferson from the same line as our James.

James and Mollie would have loved to have known this,

and they would have enjoyed seeing the finery of Virginia, but would it have changed them? No.

Mollie would have still been cooking cornbread in her wood burning stove, hoeing in her garden, and fussing at me for eating too many cherries off her tree.

After our travels through time, I started to gather all my notes and records and hoped that I had given James his significance in history. I understood after uncovering his past why it was so essential to do so.

The day I located the last piece of the puzzle to his heritage, I noticed the date in the right corner of my computer screen. It was February 3, James 160th birthday.

Coincidence? No, I don't think so. I don't begin to understand the mysteries of life and death, but I do know that folks often hear whispers of those that have passed through time.

Some try to explain those quiet voices away, and they honestly believe they are smart and logical to do so. My answer to that is that I believe in a God that can do just about any old thing He wants to do. I will acquiesce to His brilliance.

I know for a fact that the whispers of Mollie led me to so many discoveries I never knew before and led us to put a link back on a long chain.

People never really die, do they? They live on in the hearts of all those who loved them. The chain never breaks, the tie is always bound, and if you listen with faith, you can still hear them whispering.

The Curious Case Of Benjamin Walker

When I first started writing, one of my early articles was the story of my maternal Great Grandmother, The Unsinkable Mollie Sparks. Even though I adore my Mollie, she has driven me down the road toward addiction.

While trying to obtain facts for Mollie's story, I chose to look on Ancestry.com. I found the needed information for the article, but then something about her genealogy caught my eye.

Through months of digging and staring at a computer screen, I finally unmasked a treasure trove of history on Mollie's family. However, after I found her ancestors and started searching the past of other family members, I found myself becoming addicted to discovering the history of the remaining group of people I call "my relatives."

Now, I need to go to ancestryrehab.com to find a cure for my woes. Before my addiction, I was doing a reasonable job of putting the family history together. I thought it would be good for generations to come to know their roots. My goal was to compile the information into a book, thinking it would be an excellent gift for my family.

Once I finished tracing Mollie's roots, I turned my attention to other family members. I traced them with a fair amount of ease. The good news was they all wound up living in the same little town, so it became a matter of tracing steps mainly from Tennessee back through Virginia to Great Britain.

My grand plan was to research my father's family last. I knew the most about the Walker clan and thought they would be the easiest to study.

Did you know there is a 1000-page book on the Walker families? Do you know how many Walkers walked into America? However, even after testing my DNA, and researching for over a year, there is one person that is a mystery to most any Walker genealogist out there. Ah, yes, he just happens to be my curious great, great, great, great grandfather Benjamin Walker, Sr., who was born circa 1750.

Benjamin's son was Benjamin, Jr. (born 1790) and Junior's son was Andrew Jackson Walker, Sr. (born 1829) My cousin, Bob, says that he doesn't remember any word about a Benjamin, Sr.

We all know that something is amiss because I know folks who have been researching Benjamin Sr.'s roots for eighty years and still can't find his history. They have been in rehab a long time.

I decided to take the Walker family back to Benjamin Walker, Jr. and let it go. I usually don't give up, but rehab was going to be expensive. I felt sad that I couldn't go any further and find more about this frontiersman in my father's ancestry.

Two months ago, I was so frustrated with my research leading nowhere, I said aloud, "Well, Mr. Benjamin Walker if you want someone to locate you, send me a sign!" With that, I filed the notes which filled a box and put it away. Rehab averted.

On March 21, the Walker family welcomed a new baby boy into the fold. He was a surprise third baby for my nephew, David, and his wife, Denise. For three days, the poor baby had no first or middle name. For heaven's sake, they had had nine months to come up with one!

"David, what is your child's name?" I finally asked.

David gave me a silly response at first, but when he gave me his baby's real name, I was speechless.

"Aunt Lynn, it's Benjamin Jackson Walker."

David never knew about my search for our Benjamin, the grandfather of Andrew Jackson Walker.

Sometimes, when you ask for a sign, you get it.

I can't explain some of the curious mysteries of life. However, when I heard my new nephew's name, I could hear the whispers of those who lived long ago telling me to continue to search. Or was it God whispering to me to keep walking into the past so I could better appreciate my walk today?

Researching our roots is a way to get to know the family we never knew. They come alive in records and stories. We learn of the struggles and the courage it took to create our heritage and even to create a country.

I find strength when I think of my great, great, great grandmother as she crossed states in a wagon with an armful of children. I see courage when I think of the ancestors who forged west, cutting trails, farming the land, building railroads, lumber mills, and businesses. How humbled I am by the lives of relatives who died crossing an ocean, fighting in the Revolutionary War, the Civil War, the battle of the Alamo, and all other wars that followed.

Now, I must lug the notes out of the box searching, once again, for the curious Benjamin Walker, Sr. I will try my best to complete the book for the family.

After all, the old frontiersman from the past sent his namesake to forge into the frontier of the future.

It was a sign.

Clementine: "The Queen Of The Cumberlands"

In the days before cell phones, computerized cars, and microwaves lived a group of women who, as soon as they heard of someone in need, jumped into action, filling cook pots with stew to feed a hungry family, and not shying away from saddling horses in the rain. They loved God and understood giving was more important than receiving. Clemmie Copeland was such a woman.

Born in 1882 in the Cumberland mountains of Tennessee, she grew up in a one-room cabin with two glass windows, one door, seven siblings, and her parents. The heat provided during the winter came from the home's small rock fireplace.

Clemmie's mother was a striking, resolute woman respected and known throughout the Cumberlands as Aunt Hennie. Her other titles were "Herb Doctor" or "Granny Woman" because she was reputed to have delivered 1500 babies, often riding through the rugged, forested terrain to reach those in need of her services.

When the evening shadows fell through the windows, the lanterns illuminated both Clemmie and her mother using tiny pieces of cloth, a needle, and thread to create beauty from old pants, dresses, or rags. Hand stitched patchwork quilts were crafted to provide warmth for the family as well as to be gifts for others.

They spun cloth on spinning wheels or canned green beans on rainy days if they couldn't work in the fields and gardens. Their hands were never idle nor were their minds; thank goodness.

Clemmie Copeland Pugh lived 103 years. When she reached her 100th birthday, her hometown proclaimed September 12th to be Clemmie Pugh Day. Over 500 people gathered to celebrate this venerable woman who became known as the "Queen of the Cumberlands."

After Clemmie married William Pugh in 1900, she started producing more quilts. Each tiny stitch creating patterns sewn by her nimble fingers and envisioned in her inventive mind. Each became a work of treasured art.

When interviewed after her 100th birthday, the reporter asked Clemmie if it was true she had made more than 400 quilts, and she replied, "Well, I've made ever' bit of that many!" Laughing, she continued, "I always kept a quilt on hand, and then when I'd set myself down to rest, you know, I take my work up and work on the quilt."

"Did you ever sell any?" he asked.

"My son sold one, but I'd give 'um all away. My husband said I gave a good living away too. But, I never lost anything by giving folks something."

Clemmie's quilts are stunning, but what rendered them a work of art was the work of her heart. She completed eleven more quilts after her 100th birthday, all stitched by hand. Her family's rich history, photographs, and samples of her talent are displayed in the Appalachian Museum and in a book, which is still for sale throughout the country today.

My great-grandmother quilted with Clemmie at the church many an evening as a social gathering. Good friendship, lots of laughter, and hard work united these women, not to waste idle time, but to sew a stitch in time to be shared for the generations to follow. They all "took up their work" after work was done.

When I contemplate how we use our hands today compared to how we created by hand long ago, it stops me in my tracks. As my fingers glide over the keyboard to type these words, I am grateful for those who taught me, "Idle hands are useless."

Today we use our fingers to text, we use them for the remote, we twiddle our thumbs in boredom, we wring our hands in worry, and we waste time. In the generations before us, no one had time to waste. One rested while stitching or spinning, canning or cooking a pie for a sick neighbor. They gave their time freely and used their hands wisely.

Since the 1800s our lives have become physically more comfortable, and women have more freedoms. Most of us live in more than a one-room home that houses ten people. We have hospitals with obstetricians we can rush to instead of Aunt Granny. We have a Target where we can buy a quilt to keep us warm and buy green beans in a can. We park our cars on crowded, hot pavements instead of allowing our horses to cool in the shade.

However, are we happier? Could it be we are not using our idle minds and hands to create comfort or cheer for someone else? All of us, men and women, would leave our earth a better place by learning from those folks who knew with certainty,

Clemmie Pugh
circa 1972

"we never lose anything by giving folks something."

Staying busy producing joy for others fills our lives with happiness, period. If we do use our idle hands for good, we might live to be 103 and celebrate with a smile on our face, just like my Aunt Clementine,

"The Queen of the Cumberlands."

The Tie That Binds

"There she is!" I shouted to myself. I had found the old Walker Family Bible sitting in a drawer of my mother's antique wash stand. The binding was mostly gone. The book was being held together with jute twine tied in a bow.

I have always believed I have two childhood homes: LaGrange, Georgia and Monterey, Tennessee. The latter is where I was born as were all those recorded in the Bible by my great-grandmother, Lou Cynthia Ray Walker in 1879.

The history of Monterey is rich with tales of frontiersmen forging their way west. Tom Walker, Daniel Boone, President Andrew Jackson, and Davy Crockett are part of our lore.

In its heyday, Monterey became a mecca for travelers. They came first in stagecoaches, then trains and finally cars. Inns and hotels dotted the mountain welcoming visitors to the beautiful vistas and clean, crisp air.

The Monterey Lake was the home of an exclusive girl's camp in the mid-1900s, with beautiful, lush land surrounding its waters. During those days, it was open to fishing, swimming, and fun. Today, the lake is owned by several Walker cousins whom I had lost touch with over the years.

By the time we left Tennessee in the mid 60s, Monterey was a shadow of its original self. The glory days had faded and become worn like the pages of the old Bible bearing our family names. The girls' camp is long gone; most of the lake is now privately held by the Walker family. One day, after visiting my niece in Nashville, I took the back-way home to Georgia. I stopped in Monterey to put flowers on the graves of my family.

The Welch Cemetery is on a barren hillside with stones

etched with names I know as kin. I sat among the rows of gray tombstones on a hot July day and sadly realized that the boisterous, funny Walker clan was now silent.

I moved to LaGrange when I was 15, and this beautiful town on the western edge of Georgia became my second home.

On the first day of being a new student in high school, I went to my classroom and sat in front of a handsome boy named Steve. His broad smile welcomed and calmed me immediately. We became good friends, often sharing classes together. Most of the time, he sat behind me and pulled a strand of my hair. It was a reminder that I knew he always had my back.

After high school, he went on to college and then off into the world. He became very successful, and I was proud of the young man that had made me feel welcome even though we had lost touch since high school.

Last year my friend Deborah went with me to Nashville to help my sister-in-law get settled in her new home. I drove the long way to show her where I had once lived.

When we came upon the Monterey Lake and the Walker Farm, the gate was open. I decided to pull onto the dirt road that led us to the incredible acreage I had not seen in a long time.

Horses, cattle, barns, and rolling hills peacefully adorned the landscape.

A beautiful home was hiding among the hardwood trees with a gate boasting, "No trespassing!"

It was open.

"Go in.... maybe you will find a relative!" Deborah coaxed.

"Well, knowing the Walkers we could get shot!" I declared.

I stopped at the gate, unsure, but finally inched my car up the drive.

Just as I did, another car started backing out of the garage.

I hopped out of the driver's seat as fast as I could to try to stop the bullets. The man saw me approaching. He was looking at me very quizzically. Thankfully, he didn't have a gun!

"Bobby?" I timidly asked.

"Yes, can I help you?" he answered.

"It's Lynn Walker, John's sister, and your cousin."

Then as if the sky opened he knew who I was. A big hug and smiles followed.

In Bobby, I saw his father, my dad, my brother and all those that are in the old Bible and resting on that barren hillside. His hands were like my own, and his jovial nature reminded me that the Walker clan is not silent nor lost.

Since writing weekly columns for the LaGrange Daily News, Steve and I have gotten back in touch with emails and phone calls. He now lives in Nashville, where Bobby owns a home as well.

One of my stories mentioned the town of Monterey. He emailed to tell me he was just there over the weekend for a wedding.

"Were you at a lake?" I questioned.

"No, I was at a farm, why?"

"Oh nothing, my cousin Bobby owns a beautiful lake and farm there, that's all," I replied.

"What? Wait! Is your cousin an attorney in Nashville?" he questioned, surprised.

"Yes, Why?"

"He has been my corporate attorney for a while and one of the most excellent litigators I know. Plus, his son built my house!"

Blessed be the tie that binds a friend, a cousin and two childhood homes together. Just like Lou's old family Bible held together with twine, it is the blessing of the mysterious threads of our lives that ties us together complete with a beautiful bow.

These Flowers Of Love

Many cemeteries scatter over the land where I was born. Yearly, on the first Sunday in June, families unite in Tennessee to show love for those who once loved them. I don't know of a sweeter tradition than Decoration Day when folks gather to lay flowers beside stones that bear the names of their kin.

I had not been to Decoration Day in the small town of Monterey in years, but I needed to correct that. After all, beloved members of my family are laid to rest on a hill there and in the older cemetery near where the old lumber mill once stood.

I left my home in Georgia to first visit family in Knoxville. After a delightful reunion, I headed to the rural areas west, a heavenly place where the Tennessee River crosses the land of summer green, and the Great Smoky Mountains seem peaceful and serene in the distance.

In the middle of the countryside, with only one house nearby, stands a Presbyterian church built in 1797. The red brick structure with its white steeple looming to heaven is in stellar condition. Its doors still beckoning worshipers every Sunday.

The rising knoll out back holds the eternal remains of heroes who served in wars from the birth of our nation until today.

I placed an American flag in the dirt beside Revolutionary War soldier John Walker, born in 1747. I don't know how I am related to him, but DNA tells me that I am. I laid a flower beside his wife, Mary. I wondered as I walked away why I did not want to leave?

I continued west down the highway lined with limestone cliffs and crossed over the lakes and rivers to the land of the

Cumberland Plateau. I checked into my little B&B and immediately drove to gather my flowers.

My sister-in-law and her daughter were coming the next day to join me. My niece, Emily, arrived early Saturday. We set out with our coffee letting GPS direct us down a dirt path to the little Walker Cemetery. The air quickly warmed, and the bright sun filtered through the green trees that lined the way.

GPS, the Internet, and 4-wheel drive allowed us to arrive at the family graves of Andrew Jackson Walker, my great, great, grandfather born in 1829.

Of course, there was a locked chain link fence around the cemetery! After studying it for a minute, Emily and I determined we could shimmy through the gate. You would need a video to understand. I am sure the ghosts who reside there were laughing hysterically.

We planted flowers in front of A.J.'s and Clementine's graves. We studied the family around them and wondered about their lives. I questioned why I didn't want to leave?

After my sister-in-law arrived in Monterey later in the day, we drove to the cemeteries where our immediate family's names are etched in granite. We placed flowers beside grandparents, parents, siblings, husbands, fathers, aunts, uncles and cousins. The gray tombstones started to transform into rainbows.

We did the same at the older cemetery. Great-grandparents, great uncles, and a baby sister buried near a tree. My father would weep every time he would visit his little two-year-old sister's grave, so I placed a small pink flower beside her lamb-topped stone.

By the next day, the sweet flowers of love turned sadness to joy. Large groups of family members stood beside graves, told stories and rubbed headstones. The hills were alive with fragrance, bold colors, and reunion.

In an era filled with technology and futuristic thinking, perhaps we need to pause and visit the past. It is essential to teach our children that those who paved the way for tomorrow need to be honored and remembered today.

Everyone needs to return to the resting place of those who gave so much of themselves to loving us. Those who fought in wars and protected us. Those who washed off a skinned knee or read the Three Little Pigs over and over. Those who buried babies because of yellow fever, and those who cared for the churches they loved. These are the folks of our heritage. These are the stories of us.

I now know why I did not want to leave. These flowers of love had transformed death into living color. The roses, daisies, mums, and gladiolas reminded me that those I love are still alive beyond the colors of the rainbow and in my heart.

Robert E. Walker,
paternal grandfather
circa 1902

Rose Caraway Walker,
paternal grandmother
circa 1905

L to R, front row: Bill Walker, James Calvin Walker, Andrew Jackson Walker, Clementine Walker (great great grandparents) Susan Walker, Belle Walker
second row: Kate, Lou, Rosaione, Leann, Priscilla, and Hennie
back row: Jack, Joe, Bob, and Halla
circa 1885

Ruth Clementine Walker circa 1930

Monterey High School class of 1934. Ray Walker 3rd from left, front row. Elizabeth Pugh 3rd from left, second row

L to R: Dr. Paul Walker,
Ruth Clementine Walker,
Robert Walker, Ray Walker
circa 1939

L to R: Elizabeth Walker, Ray Walker, Nannie Pugh (Grandpa),
Tom Dunn, Mary Ruth Dunn, Donald Pugh, Mildred Pugh
circa 1971
(Grandpa's children and their spouses)

LaGrange

The passage of time often reveals answers to some of the "why's" we once asked. As a young Tennessee teen, I tearfully questioned my father, "Why do we have to move to Georgia now?"

If we had not moved to the idyllic west Georgia town of LaGrange in the summer of 1962, my life would not include the joy or the answers I have today.

God knew what He was doing when he placed me in the town with the beautiful fountain in the square, the imposing high school filled with fantastic friends, the college on the hill that encouraged me to write, and the local newspaper that brought me back home.

A Dream And A Poke

Dreams can come true, but it's all up to you. It doesn't matter how old you are, or even how shy or bold you are. Aspiring to achieve a goal keeps hope alive and pushes us to new heights we are meant to reach.

The real vision of seeing yourself accomplishing something you always wanted to do may be more than a dream, it may be a calling from another source.

Before I was twenty years old, I became aware of a nagging within my soul to write. When I was ten, I dreamed of dancing, at fifteen it was acting, then I was sure it was writing.

So, I became an Interior Designer.

I married, had children, divorced, married again, aged, and lived life. It was a good that God gave me the ability to be a designer because it paid the bills most of the time.

I have never heard of many dancers who could feed a few kids or help them through college. Nor do I know many actors who made it to the big time. And, writing pays nothing unless your books have sold in multitudes or Queen Oprah has blessed you.

God put me in a career to be what I was intended to be at the time I needed it in my life. It took me a while to accept that I would not be on Broadway or win a Pulitzer, but then I decided I would give my profession the best of me, and in turn, it gave me a beautiful life.

When I retired, I thought, "Ah, I can rest now! I can do whatever I want. I might finally be able to play more golf, read a book on a beach, or lay in a hammock!"

The minute I was ready to retire all things changed.

I vividly remember going to bed at night and not being able to sleep. I had a little more work to do on a large home before the curtains closed on my career stage. However, it was not the work worry keeping my eyes open.

It was as if someone was standing beside the bed and nudging me on my shoulder, almost poking me. It was aggravating.

Story topics would run through my mind. I pondered in the dark how to write this or that article. I knew that writing bug had never gone away! It had haunted me for 48 years. Now, it was keeping me up at night!

Through those years, I would write an occasional op-ed or a story, and to my surprise, they ended up in print. I knew that once I grew tired of lying on that beach during retirement, I might try writing more. It was my game plan.

Weeks passed and every night as soon as my head hit the pillow, the poking would begin. Finally, one night I said out loud, "God, if you want me to write a story you are going to have to pen the first sentence!"

I woke the next morning, and my first thought was about the old black Mercury my family owned in the early 60s.

The first sentence of the story that started my journey to finally achieving an old dream was:

"In the wee hours of an early August morning in 1962, my father's black Mercury drove onto a dimly lit, silent downtown street in LaGrange, Georgia."

I don't know how many pages I wrote in one day, but from that moment on the tapping on the keyboard never stopped. The only thing that ended was the poking.

A whole new career was born, which wasn't exactly the game plan. I intended to lie in the hammock first and then write. Oh, well, I would probably have fallen out of the dang thing anyway!

You see, it was His intent for me, not mine. We all need to listen to the purpose of God in our lives. What is it that pushes us forward? What is our calling? What do we have to do to achieve it? Is a hammock in our cards or is it something else? Do we dare try?

We are always capable of reinventing who we are. We are still the ones driving the Mercury in our lives. We just need to tune into the right voice on the radio.

I hope you always believe you can achieve more for yourself and others. Be the best you can be. May you feel a poke on your shoulder that will not stop.

It just might be the best thing that ever happened to you.

Lagrange High School Class Of 1965

In the wee hours of an early August morning in 1962, my father's black mercury drove onto a dimly lit, silent downtown street in LaGrange, Georgia. I was in the back seat peering wide-eyed through the windows trying to capture a town which would become so much a part of my future.

"Georgia? What?" I shouted as my father sat down with us earlier in the summer to tell us of the move. My parents' families settled in Tennessee even before it became a state. My grandparents were only fifty miles away, along with a gaggle of cousins, aunts, and uncles.

My mother was in the middle of building her dream home. My father was a lumberman who loved hardwoods; didn't Georgia only have pines? Plus, I had just made the junior varsity cheerleading squad! How in the world could this be happening?!

In the 60s when parents decided to relocate for their careers, the kids were expected to go with them without a fuss. My brother was graduating from college, but I was in the middle of being a teenager and absolutely certain that life was unfair.

The quiet of the car moving slowly toward this new town was eerie, yet excitement started to build. I have always known I was a nomad. Moves and adventures didn't scare me, but goodbyes were frightening. In my heart, as we left our little town in Tennessee, I knew I might never see some of my closest friends again. So the wide eyes of the fifteen-year-old in the back seat were filled not only with wonderment, but also tears.

As we approached the center of downtown LaGrange, there was a lovely little dress shop with mannequins swathed in pink in the windows. Their frozen smiles seemed warm and welcoming as the soft light bathed their faces. After fifty-three years when I remember Evelyn and Estelle's Boutique, I still think pink.

The street lights beckoned us to follow them to the central square. The centerpiece of the plaza was a beautiful illuminated fountain giving the quiet, humid air the sweet, rhythmic sound of falling drops of water. Stores, banks, and offices silently awaiting the next morning's business surrounded all four sides of the square.

I couldn't help but wonder what it would look like in the day. Would it still appear somewhat magical?

We drove around this peaceful scene toward Broad Street where I could see the outlines and evening shadows cast upon antebellum homes and stately churches. That evening in August looked as if we were traveling through a postcard. To this day when I think of LaGrange, I visit that warm summer night with clarity.

We were renting a house in the country and school would start within a month. I would be going to classes filled with unfamiliar faces at LaGrange High School. I begged God to let August slowly pass so I would have enough time to at least meet someone who would befriend me. Well, God answered big time.

The Sunday following the night we tiptoed our way into LaGrange, we attended the First Methodist Church. Dr. Bevel Jones was the pastor who took us to lunch and introduced us to many people.

The teenagers in the country where we lived drove me around town. They were all seniors but took the time to be with this new, lowly rising sophomore. I couldn't believe how friendly they were. Soon afterward, I thought, maybe life was not so unfair after all.

Within a month, I felt at home. I started school, was teased about my hillbilly accent, but was accepted anyway. I got bullied a bit, but the kindness of everyone else so overwhelmed the taunting that it became just a bother. The spirit of LHS was inspiring, and so were the classmates. I was acutely aware, even at that age, how special this place was.

The next year Mom had again built her dream home. We moved from the country into town. Folks with teenagers near my age surrounded our new home, but they were all boys! To the left was a vacant lot and Glen, who played basketball non-stop, lived in the house behind ours. Dribbling became white noise. Across the street were the Fackler brothers and that's a whole other story. Intelligent Jimmy lived beside me, and around the corner was another group of four sons known as the Mahaffey brothers. Growing testosterone surrounded me!

One afternoon I was taking a walk and heard a group of these guys playing basketball in the backyard of the Mahaffey's. I stood and watched them a while before boldly asking if I could play.

At the time, LaGrange High had no girls' basketball team, whereas Tennessee thought girls' basketball was as crucial as boys' basketball and drew as many crowds. My mother was on the state championship team as a center. She was the Mid-State Free Throw champion in the 1930s! I grew up with a basketball in my hand, and now, there were no girls to join me to shoot hoops.

Well, the minute I asked this all-male group of players if I could join the game, you would have thought I had asked them to put on dresses and dance a jig; they were dumbfounded.

Richie Mahaffey closed his mouth first and handed me the ball. I took it into my hands determined to sink a basket. It was an outside shot; it banked then dropped through the net. Thanks be to God! Richie became one of my friends forever right then, right there, and right now. What none of them knew or understood was that I had been playing basketball since I was about three, just like them.

My junior year, my friends became closer. We had shared the day of John Kennedy's assassination; we were driving, we were dating, we had experienced loss. My girlfriend's mother died tragically in early summer. The sadness in our little group still creates tears all these years later.

Heartbreaking and breathtaking was the scene as people drifted on and off Kathy's porch to pay condolences. I learned about grief that summer and how only time can ease it. I learned about faith when my friends gathered around the swing which held a mother's daughter, and we lifted her in prayer.

The fall brought football madness, homecoming dances, and drives around the Brazier Burger to see who was with whom on a Saturday night. It was the year I realized I needed to go to college and worried that I might not get in. Yikes!

I never thought of myself as smart. My mother's IQ was in the stratosphere and mine was on some rural road in Nowhereville. She was valedictorian at fifteen, and my brother was as smart as she was. I was from another planet where studying and making good grades were difficult. I would sit in the back of the class and pray the teacher wouldn't call my name. I was a teacher's nightmare, an apathetic student.

One of my first classes at LHS was biology. My teacher was Mrs. Smith, and my biology partner was one of my closest friends. I loved the course, the teacher, and Sally who helped carry me through. I made a B+ which enabled me not to have to take another science in high school since I had taken one earlier in Tennessee.

Our senior year began in 1964 with registration in the front of the school. All of us gathered and went as a group to select our classes. My mother sent me to school with a list of the least challenging courses I could take to raise my GPA.

The teachers were registering us, and when Mrs. Smith saw me, she called me to her table. I liked Mrs. Smith, so I gladly walked toward her and quickly handed her my mother's list.

She inspected the notepaper, looked up at me, and asked, " Lynn, why are you not taking my chemistry class this year?"

"Mrs. Smith, I don't need it to graduate and you know I will fail!"

Everyone knew how difficult Mrs. Smith's chemistry was. It was a legend in its own right. Even the smartest of the smart smarted over that class. Most of my friends had taken it our junior year, and I heard horror stories. The horror would also make an excellent movie if I took the class and my mother killed me!

"No, Mrs. Smith I can't take chemistry!" And, with that, she tore up my mother's note. She enrolled me in every problematic class she could think of including her horror class, chemistry.

"What are you doing?!" the panic in my voice rising as the bits of the note hit the trash.

"Lynn, I believe you are capable of more than you believe you can do. I am going to help you. You are to stay after class with me every day for six weeks. I am going to talk to your teachers and make sure they seat you in the front of their class. I will call your mother and explain to her if this doesn't work, I will pull you out of these classes and put you in the courses she requested."

At that point, I didn't know who or what to be more scared of; my mother, Mrs. Smith's chemistry class, economics, or myself!

This dear teacher saw something within me from her biology class which I did not see in myself. She believed in me when I didn't and took me under her wing. I went from an average student to an A student. I learned how to study, how to reason, how to listen, and even through design school and college I never made another lousy grade.

I became an interior designer for 43 years, owning my own business. I raised my children and helped them through college. I never looked back from that registration day in 1964, and sometimes when I think about it, I registered for life thanks to a teacher who loved her job and her students.

Our senior year was the best. We were the largest graduating class not only from our school but in the country in 1965. We WERE the war babies. Another war was raging in a far-off land called Viet Nam. We were a group bound by something other than being seniors, but I am not sure exactly what it was. Times were changing, but for us, they were the same and safe. We filled the Georgia Tech stadium to watch our team take home the State Basketball Championship. We had a fabulous prom and experienced senior moments every day. It was all pure joy.

We graduated on June 4, 1965, and we scattered to the winds. Some would go to war and not come home. Some would die in accidents or from illnesses. Some of those who were closest to me I seldom saw, and we lost touch. Some friends stayed forever, and I can pick up the phone anytime to be close to them. We had class reunions every five years and those of us who attended returned to that safe and secure place where we once lived, if only for a night.

In 2011 my 37-year-old daughter was diagnosed with breast cancer. I had lost my mother the year before and my brother and father in the late 90s. My three children were my glue and my life. My daughter had my only grandchild, and she was just six when her mother became ill. Fear spread through all of us like a giant wave getting ready to sweep us all away. It was devastating.

My first instinct was to pray. My second instinct was to ask for a lot of it. I figured I would inundate God. How could I get a lot of people to pray? I had no shame in asking anyone. I knew our class had a website to get information to others. I sent a request for prayer to my class members.

I went to school with these people for three years. My parents left LaGrange along with me in 1973, and there were no longer any ties other than memories to this beautiful town on the Georgia/Alabama line.

Within a short time after Jerry Key posted my plea, messages started coming in from all over the country. People were going to their churches asking for prayer from their congregations. Phone calls and emails poured in from these scattered war babies to help fight a war with cancer. I was amazed and thankful.

We would spend a year getting my daughter to her feet. Seven operations, infections, chemo, radiation, and tears were a part of our lives. I watched my granddaughter have to accept a new kind of grown-up world that she was unprepared for but, with God's grace, she kept her joy.

My son suffered a severe injury in 2014, and again, I turned to my old class for prayer. These extraordinary folks responded, and God answered as well by healing both of my children.

I said before that I didn't know what it was that made this class special, but I do now. It is the group of individual, beautiful people who comprised the whole class. We walked together through one of life's crucial growing times. We leaned on each other as we journeyed through and we lean on each other now. The laughter, the joy, the safe place, the teachers that aided us became memories that we, as a class, will share for all our days.

When I look back to that ride in the back seat of the Mercury and my eyes settling on the pink ladies in the window, I realize I did not know that I was on the road to not only an adventure but a part of God's path for me and His amazing grace.

Right before my mother died, she wanted me to take her to LaGrange. We drove through the memories, around our old home, the stately square, the church, and with tears, she said, "It was one of the best places I ever lived." And I simply replied, "Me too, Mom, me too."

a few classmates
from the class of
1965

The Reunion

Reunions, whether they are family or class, lift one's soul. They warm us with memories which were hidden and suddenly brought back to life. These gatherings make us wish we could stay longer, hug tighter, and hold on to the people who made such a difference in our world.

Our 50th High School reunion was on a warm October evening in LaGrange, Georgia. A large crowd gathered to return to a time that filled a lot of our days with laughter. I suddenly was seventeen again. Although I have to admit, I have never acted very grown up.

Yes, age has changed us. The hair is grayer or balder, the skin not as smooth, and the bodies not as toned. But once you see past the age, there is the seventeen-year-old with the same smile, the same twinkle in the eye, and the same heart.

People surprise you at reunions. We often wonder why close friends at seventeen seem to forget us as the years pass. I was standing watching a video of classmates depicting the changes in us through the years. One of my best friends couldn't be at our reunion and was facing some challenges ahead with his health. When his picture came on the screen, I looked for a minute and then couldn't watch anymore. Tears filled my eyes, and I needed to turn away.

The room was dark. I reached for a napkin to dry my eyes and not make a scene. Suddenly I felt someone behind me, turn me around, and just hold on to me. I haven't seen this incredible old friend much in the last fifty years, but she knew what I was feeling, understood and hugged me. Some friendships come back just like that. We were never forgotten.

Approximately 18% of our class is gone. When we watched a memorial video of those smiling faces who once walked the school halls with us, you could hear a pin drop and a tear fall in the room. In five more years the percentage of those gone will grow, but for this one night, we were here enjoying one another and being very appreciative of the friends who are still with us.

As folks started to leave, I was sitting at a table with a friend of mine and asked, "Alec, why are they leaving?"

With his dry humor and his eyes fixated on the door, he answered, "I don't know, but I know I will be a little depressed tomorrow. I always am after one of these reunions."

I understood all too well how Alec felt. I am always sad as well. Perhaps we realize we were able to visit those who traveled with us through an era. We try to catch up many years in a night, and it is an impossible task. About five of us stayed until they removed the last napkins from all tables. We honestly tried.

Reunions have a reason for being. We are reuniting with people who mean the world to us. They give us an occasion to do so and say, "I love you, thank you, and I haven't forgotten you."

The next time you receive an invitation to a reunion of any kind, GO! It is God's way of reminding you that loved ones will always be there with a smile, a hug, and a pocketful of memories.

The Year Of Being A Senior

Often, when I am starting my Sunday mornings with a hot cup of coffee, I wonder what the subject of my next column should be. The brain is complicated, and mine is full of broken subjects and sentences that whirl around trying to find structure.

Usually, when I feel my brain has jumped track, I take my Sunday morning walk and converse with God. By the time I am into my first mile, a theme for a story will start to form. Today, however, all my thoughts were just a collection of mumbo-jumbo.

A white car passed me near my home, going a bit too fast.

"Teenagers!" I thought.

As it flew by me, I noticed letters printed on the rear-view window in multi colors:

"SENIOR! '18!" Yes, a speeding 17-year-old on their way to the last year of high school.

I smiled. I knew God just gave me my story.

An email came across my computer the other day. You know how you can receive a letter or a message that lifts your spirits and makes your day? Well, that email was one of those.

It seems our high school class has decided since we are all turning seventy this year, we might be getting too old to have a reunion once every five years. Duh! Of course, we are.

We have lost some dear classmates over the years and, of course, as we age, our class size dramatically declines. It is a sad thought, but one that is just plain realistic. Sometimes realism is traumatic.

I still pass a mirror and wonder whose image it is reflecting.

Trauma is when I realize it is me! My soul is still a senior at LaGrange High. My reflection should reveal that!

I think most of my class of seventy-year-old folks feel the same way. At least we are getting a bit smarter by trying to get together sooner rather than later. Duh! Of, course we are.

Many of us live in other cities, other states and are busy living our lives. There are schedules, football games, conflicts, and families pulling and tugging us to go in a thousand different directions and gaze into a thousand different mirrors.

I don't know how many our class can gather in a short amount of time, but my theory is that I should get a bus and round them all up. May have to hog tie a few, but I am still strong, so that doesn't scare me.

If I can't find a bus or my rope, I will get my car, pick up Marie and head to LaGrange. There is nothing like riding in a vehicle with Marie. She can turn a frown to a smile with her magic humor. She has not changed a bit since seventeen. Same dry wit, same kind heart, same beautiful person, and, doggone, she is the same size!!

How little do we change from those folks we were in 1965? I am still me. I am a bit wiser, have a few thousand more wrinkles, and have no idea what happened to the body where I once lived.

As the teen's car passed me on the road today, I realized I should have waved her down, made her stop, and told her a thing or two.

"Honey, don't speed through life. It goes fast enough without putting your foot down on the peddle. It was just yesterday I was starting my senior year with some great friends. Now my great friends and I truly are seniors.

"Yes, you are looking at the wrinkles and the body that you will one day own. Yes, honey, you will not look the same; however, a part of you will never age. It is the part that still dances, still laughs and keeps you wanting to gather old friends on a drive down the road."

I am going to get my bus, grab my pals, and write on the rear-view window in bold colors, "SENIORS! '65!"

Marie and I will laugh as we speed toward our reunion. We will not be racing to get to the future; we will be rushing to reunite with the past. Time is of the essence.

Duh! Of course, it is!

Friends

"Greater love has no one than this, that someone lay down his life for his friends." John: 15:13

Friends are bonus gifts from God. Whether you know a friend for a day, for a few years, or for a lifetime, they are all blessings.

When rain falls in our lives, our pals try to find the sun. When an embrace, or an ear, or a pat on the back is needed, they provide.

Friends are the angels who give us wings to fly, laughter to fill our hearts, and comfort to warm our souls.

They are the colorful ribbons of love.

Retying The Ribbons

I have often thought of friends as ribbons that run through our lives; bright-colored trimmings that wrap around their gifts of joy, love, sanctuary, and understanding.

Those ribbons form a quilt to warm our soul when the storms come and brighten our hearts when all else seems dark.

What would we do without them?

When I was six, I lived on a farm outside Nashville, Tennessee. My father rented a house on this property for two years while he helped his brother launch a new business.

Mr. Fowler, the owner of this vast farmland, was a person I shall never forget. His sizeable, yet cozy, house sat on a hill, surrounded by white fences, a swimming pool, guest house, red barns and Tennessee Walking horses. Most who knew him also knew his compassionate heart and gentle nature.

The property superintendent was Mr. King. He and his family took care of the farm because this fairytale place was just a weekend retreat for the Fowler family.

Mr. King's daughter, Edna, was age seven. Mr. Fowler's daughter, Mary, was age five. Edna and Mary fought all the time. If Edna wanted to ride horses, Mary wanted to ride bikes. If we were playing in Mary's house, Mary bossed us both which angered Edna. I became the anointed peacemaker because I adored them both. However, when my skills failed and the bickering grew to a fever pitch, Mary's parents would intervene and toss us all outside or send us home.

I learned a lot about friendship in those two years. I learned never to bully, never to let money be a factor in choosing friends, and that you can love a lot of different folks even if you don't always agree with what they do.

One day, Mr. Fowler sent his butler down the hill to bring me to the big house, where Mr. Fowler greeted me. "Lynn, I have a surprise for you!"

Mary was not there, but her mother was. Mrs. Fowler came out of the kitchen holding a box.

When I opened it, there, lying in the folds of tissue paper, was a pair of black patent Mary Jane shoes. I had forever admired them in the window of Red Rooster Shoes in Nashville.

I screeched, jumped up and down, and went on for a minute like a chimp in a zoo.

Finally, I calmed down, realizing it wasn't my birthday or Christmas, and then exclaimed, "How did you know I love these shoes?"

"Lynn, I called your Mom and asked her what you would like to have as a gift. Once she told me, I bought these for you."

"Mr. Fowler, why did you buy them? It is not my birthday?" I exclaimed.

He knelt, looked into my eyes, and gently said, "I wanted to reward you for your understanding of true friendship."

I didn't comprehend what he meant until many years later.

William Sydney Porter, better known as the writer O. Henry, once said,

"No friendship is an accident."

I couldn't agree more. I believe God gives us our friends as part of a master plan to shape, guide, and help us move through the journey of life.

There are those we meet when we are young who remain a constant presence in our lives. They are rare and few. Those ribbons of friendship are tied so tight that you cannot imagine life without their binds.

I met someone in my teen years who became a good friend. We were an unlikely pair. He was a guy for one thing, so that made it different. Even though I had terrific girlfriends, this friendship was somehow unique.

We married others, moved apart, lived entirely separate lives, yet we always found the time to catch up.

This "unlikely pair" have known each other well for over fifty years. We see each other rarely, but then we are rare. My friend has always been there for me, and I for him. He was just simply, "God chosen." There is something profound when you know, with absolute certainty, nothing can untie this type of ribbon.

Some ribbons slip away, but that doesn't make them any less unique. They are never forgotten, never unappreciated because they are essential to our lives.

As we age, most of us look back to those who made our lives rich and colorful, and we often want to re-tie the ribbons.

When our high school class of 1965 met for our 50th reunion, there seemed to be a greater need for us to reconnect than there had been at past gatherings.

Our class has always been close, but this time I just wanted to grab all those high school seniors and take them home! Something was different.

Over the past few years, this same group has been reaching out more on social media to stay connected. When one in our class stumbles or needs prayer, the word travels immediately, and we fall to our collective knees. We all share part of a life journey and memories. We know we have had an impact on each other's lives in some way.

We are retying the ribbons.

When we reconnect to those who have slipped away from our present lives, we, most of the time, get sprinkled with a bit of magic dust.

After just a moment or two, the years and distances fade away, and we just pick up where we left off. We don't even notice age. We only see that bright colored spirit meeting up, once again, with our hearts.

I can't imagine where I would be without the love, forgiveness, laughter, strength, sharing, encouragement, criticism, and prayers from my friends today and those of long ago.

When I think of friendship, I often recall those early days back on the Fowler farm. I can see Edna, Mary, and me holding hands as we walk the path to the big house in the bright summer sun.

The gift of a friend is priceless, and the memory of a friend is ageless. I thank God for those who have shared a path with me. You are the ribbons that give my life color and immense joy.

What would I do without you?

Angels Sent To Write The Story

Do we ever get too old for life not to surprise, excite, or tease us? Are we ever allowed to let age keep us from trying new beginnings or mastering an old challenge? What is it that pushes some to always move toward a new chapter and others to wait for an end?

I have learned so much over the last few years; more than I could have possibly dreamed—all because I heard a voice. I confess I am a terrible listener; however, the one time I decided to pay attention was the right time. When God pulls you close and yells in your ear to the point there is ringing for days, you listen.

After retiring from a long career in design, a new career began when I opened my ears. I instinctively knew I would be rushing to finish sentences and working to reshape words until the day I leave this earth. I knew some would view my new path as a possible precursor to a brain illness or some other malady that befalls folks my age. Even with their doubts as well as my own, I pressed on.

However, I could never continue without my angels.

When I recall how this new career began over two years ago, it seems surreal. An adopted hometown returned me to the newspaper I read as a teen. LaGrange Daily News published the first line of my first story. Of course, God wanted it to be about LaGrange. Why not? He and I both know the town is unique.

After over 100,000 words formed sentences which turned into stories and transformed into weekly articles, I know many LaGrange citizens are angels.

Those same words have traveled across the country introducing me to people from New Hampshire to Iowa, Colorado to Washington State and places in between. Sentences have forged friendships with folks whom I will never meet, but I shall always remember.

An angel left a gift in my mailbox at Christmas. On the cover of a small notebook is a quote by Ernest Hemingway. Every time I begin to write I read Hemingway's words, "There is nothing to writing. All you do is sit down at a typewriter and bleed." Hemingway had a way with words that touches my heart, but the kindness of the angel who gave the gift embraces my soul.

Former teachers, dear old friends, new friends, and family, not only in LaGrange but elsewhere, lifting me and telling me to always, "keep writing" are angels.

When we listen to God's expectations for us and try our best to achieve them, you can bet God will send us angels to guide our paths. These angels are the friends who will always hold our hands to support, encourage, and inspire us.

I received an email this week from a publisher who needed an article about spring fashion and the mature woman. I know as much about style as I do about Algebra; I failed Algebra.

However, I know the spirit of the women who are my stylish friends. I had an idea. I called these four extraordinary neighbors and asked if they could help me with a new story idea for a column.

I gave them very little time to prepare, yet they showed up dressed in spring attire, ready for their pictures to be taken surrounded by tulips, even as the cool spring air turned their lips purple. Words came easily for the story about ageless angels dressed as friends in current spring fashions.

When I write in the silence of my space, I listen to the noises of my life. I hear the children when they were little and the grandparents of long ago. I am keenly aware of friends as their angel wings flutter around me. Each person who crosses my life's path is unique, exquisite, and a beautiful blessing. These gifts are my reason there is a story to tell.

I am amazed how words have given me a gift which mere words cannot describe. Just because I retired after forty-three years doesn't mean my life's work was near its end; a new chapter was beginning.

All of us have new chapters. Each person is called to continue to strive, to share, to make a difference until the day we take our last breath.

Listen carefully to instructions for the next chapter in your life. You might be amazed by the angels you meet and how much you appreciate them. Live every day expecting it to surprise you, excite you and for sure, keep your ears open.

The Ladies Who Lunched

A friend of mine said to me recently, "When you go back to visit high school friends you can't pretend to be something you are not because they all knew who you were!"

His statement stuck with me because it is true. We all travel through years of living, moving, growing, and changing. However, I have learned that if you look carefully, the core of the person you once knew is still the same.

I am sure there are exceptions of course because life, love, and war can severely alter a human being. However, there are some who can weather life, love, and war while still being true to who they always were.

Such was the case with the ladies who lunched on a chilly December day in 2015.

We had gathered at our class reunion a few months before. While there, the four of us promised to meet again. "Maybe lunch." We all say those type of things before we leave reunions, but most of the time our individual lives take over and we never quite make plans

The four of us were close in high school at one time or another, but over the years, the closeness was being erased by distance and years. Could we catch up; could we go back and visit the person we once knew well?

The older we get, the more we want to reach back and grab onto the past. Revisit, rekindle, and return to find out how folks we were once close to are doing now. How had their lives turned out? Has life changed them? Did their hearts survive and their souls remain intact through the ups and downs of life?

The Ladies who Lunched that December day have a mutual friend in crisis. When crises happen, we are all reminded how fleeting time can be. We come face to face with our mortality and realize that lunch plans suddenly require more planning.

On that chilly day we gathered at my home promptly at noon. The Christmas lights sparkled on the big tree, the table set, and the lunch prepared. After heartfelt hugs we gathered to give thanks, holding hands sitting around the candlelit table.

As I looked at their faces, I reflected on each one of my old friends. If I had to give a one-word description of Ree in high school and now, it would be "regal." Tall, beautiful, and always poised, she was one of the first friends I made when I moved to LaGrange, Georgia in 1962.

Kindness overflows her soul. I can't remember one thing she ever said or did that was unkind. Not one. She didn't gossip or pass judgment on anyone. I always admired her.

After high school, Ree and I drifted apart. We were different, but I think we appreciated our diversity. I know I did.

Marie is still adorable, petit, and joyful. Her one-word description would be "friend." It is incredible how she loves folks. Her sense of humor could put a hardened soul at ease. I love her quick wit and how she can take hardship and turn it into a funny moment.

I know she uses her humor in telling you about her life; however, she does so in order to not evoke pity or sadness. Marie is one of the most understanding people I know. I could say anything to her, and have. When I think of her, a smile always accompanies my thoughts.

Jo is sitting across from me at the table. "Happy" is the word to describe her. She radiates it. Her smile could light the Christmas tree and will brighten any room, anywhere.

I became closer to Jo before my senior year. We stayed in touch through the first years of our marriages and then life took us on different journeys.

If I had tried to predict Jo's future in high school, I would never have conjured the scenario which unfolded. She married young to another high school buddy who became a minister. She and Dan have traveled far and spread seeds of joy wherever they go. Their lives are full and fruitful. Their love is constant and inspiring.

As I observed these old friends, I noticed something incredible.

I knew many of their personal stories. I knew they had all suffered incredible loss and moments of gut-wrenching trials. So had I. However, here we were—laughing and talking despite it all!

The storms of life had not changed these lovely women. Sorrows had not defined them, but strengthened them instead, and it shows. Each one has tremendous faith and is in awe of God's brilliance.

People assume you can't revisit the past. I say you can. If you do, you just might be surprised at the joy you find. You might be overwhelmed by the spirit of friendship and love. You might also be astonished to learn that some people are not the same that they were in high school, some are even better. Some are more kind and regal, some are even better friends, and some will just make you happy.

Just like the ladies who lunched.

Beauty In The "Bunko Babes"

Envisioning the game of Bunko often conjures up women with blue hair rolling dice, and straining to see how many little dots appear. But in reality, it's just a mindless game of luck. Mostly, it's an excuse for a group of women to get together, laugh, and gab.

It has been nine years since I first became a bona fide dice thrower. Back then our Bunko was run by Iron Fisted Ellen: the keeper of the key, and the rules; the boss that kept the group from falling into chaos.

Courageous Ellen passed away from cancer several years back.

When our group of Bunko girls can't remember the rules, we all envision Ellen, arms folded, looking up at the Lord saying,

"They are just not right, Sir. I tried."

"I know, Ellen, I know..." as He strolls away shaking His head.

The last time we gathered we were minus one player. Most didn't want to play the game at all. It seemed they would rather sit around, having several conversations going all at once.

I settled on the floor as Darlene asked the group, "Well, are we going to play or are we going to talk? It doesn't matter to me."

"I have an idea!" My mouth spoke before my brain had fully developed the thought.

"Why don't we go around the group and find out what each person would like to accomplish within a year. What is it that you would like to finish or would like to try but have been putting off?"

My Bunko group consists of ladies who are mostly retired, between the ages of 60 and 80 but still have a sparkle in their eyes and a gleam in their hearts. They live comfortably, have worked hard, and have experienced a myriad of tragedies and joys. They are the culmination of their many experiences in life.

As my idea caught on among the group, I realized we might have some funny, thoughtful, even provocative answers, so I grabbed a notepad.

Arlene was first. She should have been a comedian. Philadelphia born and raised and always evoking fun.

"I have always wanted to work with children who are sick, or abused, or just need love."

Within a few moments, she had names of agencies to contact and people to call who could help her achieve that long-awaited goal.

Martha sat to the left of Arlene. "I am older and not as fit as I once was, but I do all I can. I will continue to stay active so that I can continue my work with the Assistance League of Atlanta."

Connie then started to speak. Her daughter has been fighting life-threatening cancer for quite a while. I understand when insurmountable pain accompanies you daily; one views life with different glasses.

Her response, "I want to continue to help those who I love. They all know I need hearing aids. I am finally going to get them!"

Connie took a simple problem from her complex world to change her life as well as others. Connie decided to help her family as well as herself because she realized vanity has no room next to love.

Darlene, our host, then spoke. "I am going to continue to be dedicated to caring for my husband whom I love."

Darlene has been caring for an ailing Wyn for a while. She does so with grace, bravado, and style that never evokes pity, but instead admiration.

Deborah is my non-blood sister. I think I know most things about her, but then she can surprise me.

"I want to reconnect with old friends."

Deborah, having her Deborah personality, has about a thousand friends now, so she must be going for a Guinness record.

She continued, "I want to keep volunteering at the nursing home, working with disabled adults, and get re-involved in a Bible Study group."

Deborah will not have to stand in line at the Pearly gates because Heaven has mailed her a key.

Ricki chooses a new word every year to continue to grow. "This year my word is transformation. Transform my health as well as my spirit so that I can continue to help my eleven grandchildren."

Ricki doesn't know it, but I can guarantee, there are at least eleven people transforming into extraordinary humans because of this beautiful woman.

Virgie, new to the Babes this year, has her word, "patience." Toward the end of her teaching career, she noticed her patience was dwindling. She knew it was time to retire. Now she wants to renew the patience she once had and apply it to all aspects of her life. A teacher never stops learning.

Barbara trains service dogs for others. She and her dog, Zoey, go to the Children's Hospital weekly so that Zoey can comfort the most vulnerable among us. Barbara needed to add nothing to her tomorrow, except to continue the great work she is doing today.

Judy is a cancer survivor, a grandmother who looks like a model. Her retirement days are just around the corner. She, too, wants to work with children. She also wants to spend more time with her children, grandchildren, and daughter-in-law.

Her life has not been without trials, but I have never heard her complain. Now all she wants to do is not sit down, but to just love.

Another Judy sits beside her. A fireball, fun-loving, happy

woman. Not yet retired.

"My goals are not lofty or heroic, but I want to smile at folks more. The strangers in line with me at the grocery or to anyone I pass. I want to share kindness."

Then it was my turn.

I want to write about the folks who call themselves Seniors who are always willing to find avenues to grow, to help, to love, to give, to better themselves.

We are more than blue hairs. We are blondes, brunettes, redheads, fit, capable, and still laughing. Beneath the laughter is a richness that has been attained only through the art of living.

Meanwhile, in Heaven, the Lord returns to Ellen's side after listening to the Bunko Babes.

"Ellen, what do you think of those girls now?" the Lord asked as He tapped her crossed arms.

"Impressive!" she said as she relaxed her fist. "However, Sir, they still need to learn those rules!"

I could swear I heard laughter somewhere in the heavens above me.

Apron Strings And Jimmy Choo Shoes

My mother was sitting at her sewing machine as I walked into the kitchen. This activity was not an unusual sight. She was a fabulous seamstress and could turn the simplest patterns into masterpieces.

"What are you making, Mom?" I inquired.

"Oh, I had some scraps of fabrics and thought I would make a few aprons. Mine are looking tired," she replied as she stitched away.

My mother never entered the kitchen without wearing an apron. Neither did my grandmother, my great-grandmother, and any grandmothers before that. Aprons were as important a staple as a frying pan.

Until the day she died, whenever I prepared a meal, my mother would ask, "Where is your apron?" She would then reach into my pantry, find an apron and tie one around my waist.

"Why take a chance you could ruin your clothes?" she would say. And, of course, I had no answer.

After Mom passed away, I was going through her things. I found the drawer where the aprons lay neatly waiting to be touched again with those loving hands.

I picked them up one by one and studied the detail. Mama had hand cross-stitched a design along the hemline and pocket of one. Another one had patch-worked fabrics and lace. All of them were wonderfully made and as precious as a $1000.00 pair of Jimmy Choo shoes or a Prada bag.

Michele is my friend who was getting ready to celebrate a birthday. There are a few of us who still buy each other a small gift when we turn a page on age. We like to make our birthdays a bit special, so Michele, Deborah, Ricki and I went to lunch.

We drove to the birthday girl's restaurant of choice. A French café is in the heart of the ritzy Buckhead Shops of Atlanta. Expensive hotels, fine dining, and the stores of Prada, Gucci, and of course, Jimmy Choo shoes surround the French bistro.

As we dined on the patio, we watched a parade of luxury cars, as well as luxuriously clad people of all ages, pass.

Michele's heritage is part French. She can even speak a bit of the language. She is a tiny thing with impeccable taste. Reared in New England, schooled in the west and raised in all things proper. She became an executive for a major company out of college and retired from the same company. Her glass ceiling shattered before the rest of us understood what that even meant.

Michele's clothes are of the most excellent quality with an array of purses and jewelry which always coordinate. She was right at home sitting amid the beautiful shops and the exquisite food of the French café.

As she reached to open her present from me, I wondered why in the world I would give her the gift resting in the black and white wrapped box.

I had gotten the old sewing machine out a few weeks prior and decided to make an apron or two. A lost art. Since Michele had everything, I thought at the time, this would be something different and possibly something she did not own.

Yes, you can buy an apron for a song, but not the ones like my mama made or my grandmother, or my great grandmother. No, "homemade" is the real apron. Don't ask me why, but they work better.

I selected a French fabric with shades of rose, black, and green. I carefully applied trims and gathered the skirt. I centered designs and cut it shorter for my petite friend. I pressed, folded, and wrapped it in white tissue and placed it in the box.

Now, as I was sitting among the glitter of midtown Atlanta,

I felt that possibly I had the wrong gift for Michele. What was I thinking?!

After our delicious meal, she opened her present. Her eyes lit up, and she exclaimed she loved it. She held it up to look at it, smiled, and then put it in her large, beautiful purse.

After we ate, we started walking around to the various shops and window dreaming.

We turned the corner, and Michele walked right through the doors marked "Jimmy Choo." We all followed. I stood in the center of this small shop and gazed at all the elegantly displayed shoes on every glass shelf. My mouth was wide open.

The shoes were enticing me with their beauty. When I picked one up and saw the price, I almost dropped it. However, I could see why they were treasures to those who could afford them.

"I have a pair on, and I love them!" Michele said as if she were walking around in a pair of tennis shoes.

For the rest of the afternoon, I made a mindful promise to not step on Michele's Jimmy Choos!

As we started home, we decided to stop for coffee at the Starbucks near our houses. You can run into a lot of people you know in this little shopping center.

Michele was sitting in the back seat rummaging through her purse and pulled out the apron.

"What are you doing?" I shockingly stated as she stepped out of the car and tied on her apron.

"I want to see what it looks like on me!"

Truthfully, it looked adorable and fit perfectly.

"Well, I love it so much I am going to wear it!" she said emphatically.

So, off went little Michele in her Jimmy Choo wedges wearing her handmade apron through the shops near our homes with not a worry in the world. Proper was out the window.

Magnificent were the shoes, precious was the apron, beautiful was the birthday girl who abandoned all that was normal for her, to celebrate friendship joyously.

With a twinkle in her eye, Mama would have proudly tied the French apron strings around Michele's waist while proclaiming, "Why take a chance of ruining those Jimmy Choo shoes?"

Shadows

The shadow I once feared forced me to examine many aspects of life. I gained insight and compassion while in the darkness of depression. When people suffer from an illness which is not visible, we still need a doctor, a loving family, and friends who can see our need.

As my brain began to heal, my faith grew, my love deepened, and bravery overcame weakness. It will always be my mission to share the story of my struggles so that others will understand their own.

Would I be who I am without the shadow accompanying me? I doubt it.

This chapter is dedicated to:
Dr. William Theron McLarty

No Fear Of The Shadow

She was on the playground in front of her school. The old, three-story brick building with the spiraled, orange fire escape loomed over the dirt schoolyard. She was the bride in a mock wedding performance held by her class on the sidewalk. She was eight; her groom, Martin, was the same age.

The spring air blew strands of wispy blond hair around her face as she walked toward Martin. The little girl was excited that she was the bride walking the sun-soaked path toward the make-believe altar.

Then, as if the day turned to night and as quickly as a smile can turn into a frown, she felt strangely alone and awkwardly out of place. The last thing she saw before falling on the concrete was the blurred brick building with the orange fire escape melting into the dirt below. Anna had fainted.

Anna would have similar episodes in the years that followed. A feeling the world was far away. A world where people walked in one direction and her, another. There were days when she would feel lost as if she were alone in a crowded schoolyard.

Finally, one day while happily at work in her twenties, Anna again fell to the floor. An ambulance came. Before the day was over, she found herself in a strange room, talking to a stranger. His name was Dr. McLarty, a leading psychiatrist in the treatment of depression and other brain illnesses.

Dr. McLarty was to Anna, a calm hand on a shaken soul, a kind man who asked gentle questions in order to learn who she was and how she felt. Anna started to talk and was surprised as the words fell out and around and all over the room.

His eyes grew larger as she explained, and he would learn that the little girl with the wispy blonde hair had been living with a shadow all her life. The shadow's name was "Depression."

I met this little girl the day I was born. You see my name is Anna Lynn. It is a day of bravery when I can share with you this story. God and time make fear fade.

When you reach the latter part of your life, you realize what is important is helping others. If you can do so with your own story, then do it. That is where I am today.

Once I was diagnosed with clinical depression, (an imbalance of chemicals in the brain) I was given a variety of drugs, but none worked. Instead, my treatment was a regimen of counseling and jogging. For fifteen years I ran hard to place myself in front of the shadow.

Depression, like many brain illnesses, is treated with trial and error. Some treatments work, and some don't. I call them "brain" illnesses instead of mental illnesses because of the connotation of the word "mental."

All my life, I have heard folks talking about illnesses of the brain. "People need to buck up." "I don't believe in psychiatrists!" "How could anyone be so selfish to commit suicide?" "People just need to believe in God more."

Let me tell you from experience, you can have the courage of a lion and still feel weak in the dimness of the shadow. If you don't believe in a psychiatrist for the brain, then don't go to a cardiologist for your heart.

Depression causes suicide often because the depressed person feels the most unselfish thing he/she can do is leave this earth and not be a bother anymore. Their thinking is from their troubled mind, not yours.

And finally, God is the one that knows your hurting brain and is trying to help you get the aid needed. Did he not create the doctor to help your heart? If so, then he created the psychiatrist to help your brain.

If you are experiencing either situational or clinical depression or just an emptiness that doesn't go away, please understand you CAN be better, and there is hope. Seek help. Brain illness is NOT your fault.

There should be no stigma any longer for brain dysfunction. Instead, we need to encourage ones who could be in trouble to seek help, to lend understanding, and finally, to support and never judge.

Dr. McLarty wanted to try one newer drug for me years ago. I balked at the idea, but I took it every morning for three weeks doubting it would work.

I was sitting at my l breakfast table on a very sunny, Sunday morning, reading the paper and drinking a cup of hot coffee. Suddenly, out of nowhere and not thinking about a thing, I physically felt a veil was lifted off me from the bottom of my feet to the top of my head.

When I explained the sensation later to Dr. McLarty, he smiled a broad smile. "That phenomenon has been reported before in rare cases of those who have lived years with depression. Once the chemicals in the brain are balanced, it can produce a euphoric phenomenon."

Many years have now passed. I take one pill a day, see my gentle doctor once every two years, and the shadow stays behind me.

The courage to seek help, the love of three beautiful children, and the love of a God who whispers in my ear, "Fear not, for I am with you…always" has kept me playing on this noisy schoolyard called life.

No Parking Available At The Psychiatrist's Office

As most of you are aware, I never shy away from writing about or discussing the frailties of my personal life. Most of you have read my articles regarding my journey with depression and anxiety.

Many readers, as well as friends, will often say, "Lynn, you are so brave to tell your story!" Others will ask, "Why do you share your struggles?"

My answers are simple: There is no bravery involved because I am not ashamed of the crosses I bear. If we do not share with others our travails, then how do others understand their own?

Several weeks ago, my answering machine recorded a message from an old friend of mine. "Lynn, it's Dr. McLarty calling. I haven't seen you in a while, and it's time to check in. Call me."

Dr. McLarty is the psychiatrist who first treated me in the late 1970s. He is still practicing, still my doctor, and still provides the medicine I require to combat clinical depression. We see each other every two years, but this time we both were past due for a check in and checkup.

For forty years, this healing man has guided me through some horrific storms and believed in my strength, my faith, and my desire to ease the illness I have carried since I was seven.

Last week I drove to Ridgeview Institute in Atlanta where my good doctor has kept his office all these years. It had been more than two years since I parked my car in front of his building; except this time, there was no parking available.

Ridgeview has grown into a small campus situated over 37

acres with ten buildings. Youth and adults of all ages and professions arrive on its grounds searching for relief from addiction or mental health issues.

"Lynn! Finally, I get to see you!" Dr. McLarty greeted me with a big bear hug and accompanying smile.

"What is with all the cars out there, buddy?" I immediately asked.

"Ah, just folks needing help," he replied in a noticeably reticent tone.

His office was the same. Same pictures, same chairs, and same paper disarray on his desk. The large room needs redecorating badly, but something is comforting about returning to a place which provided years of refuge from the chaos of my cluttered mind.

He laughed as we discussed my world of writing. "I knew you would always do what you are doing now! I knew it!" I failed to mention, McLarty is also my cheerleader with pep squad credentials.

Our meeting lasted the usual hour. We found my brain is normal for me, and my medicine would stay the same. Check-up finished. I was overjoyed to see my friend and was astonished he was continuing to offer a healing hand to those who suffer from depression, bipolar disorder, addictions, anxiety, all other personality abnormalities and suicidal tendencies.

As I drove away, I was dodging folks strolling, the cars vying for my parking place and noticing the teens as well as adults leaving one building to walk to the next. My joy faded as I realized how many needed mental health care and how many had just begun their journey onto the long path to wellness.

Dr. McLarty and those who could have retired long ago are still practicing because they are desperately needed. Right now, there are six times the individuals who need help to one mental health care worker including all psychiatrists, psychologists, counselors, psych nurses, and social workers combined. More than 56% of adult Americans who have a disorder receive no or inadequate treatment.

Youth with severe depression rose from 5.9% to 8.2% from 2012 to 2015, with 76% of those young folks having no or inadequate treatment. Teen and youth suicide rates are rising, fueled by pressure from peers, parents, society, social media, abuse, and a myriad of other issues.*

We often have the tendency to put out heads in the sand when faced with uncomfortable subjects we do not understand. Mental health is one of them. However, it shouldn't be since one in five people suffer from some form of psychological disturbance.

I often ask myself why so many do not ask for help. It is perplexing to me that when we suffer from pain anywhere in our body, we run to the doctor, but when we suffer from pain within our soul, we run into a closet. How sad is that?

So many stay quietly in despair because they do not want to trouble their family or friends, or their false pride is killing their truth. I understood long ago the only way to unburden those I love was to seek help, so they no longer had to deal with the mess in the closet.

It took work, patience, God, a doctor, and a loving family to transform me into being all I was intended to become. Long ago the medicines offered did not work for me, but the help I received through therapy saved my life. I was lucky when Dr. McLarty finally found the right medication for my brain so it no longer wants to thrust me into darkness.

There is no bravery involved, nor embarrassment in telling my story. I choose not to hide in a closet or look for a sandbox in which to bury my head. My earnest prayer is that you don't either.

***MHA, The State of Mental Health in America, 2018**

A Prescription For The Blues Brothers

I was in the middle of experiencing days of the blues and blahs. The only comfort I found was lying on my sofa.

I had no reason to feel that way. The week before the blues started, I had just returned from a whirlwind two-week vacation with my family. After returning home I finished off some yummy chocolate, washed all the clothes, and sorted the mail. Then I visited and laughed with some precious friends I missed while gone. So, why was I down?

Usually, when I fly home after visiting my children in south Florida or Colorado, I get a sinking feeling. Leaving my children and grandchild is never fun. I go under for a day or two, but then I pull myself out of the water, dry off, and enjoy the sun.

From someone who suffers from clinical depression, I do have to be cautious. Upsetting thoughts can run through my head. "Did I take my medicine?" "Is my medicine broken?" Why am I not getting better?" "I need to call the doctor!"

I started the week home from vacation by writing my column for the paper which usually makes both my editor and me happy. No, not this time. Mr. Blue had parked himself in a chair beside my desk and impatiently waited for me to finish so we could return to the sofa.

"Maybe I just need some quiet time, and all will be well," I whispered to myself.

I drove to Barnes and Noble, sat with my Starbuck's Americana and listened to pages turning as soft music played in the background. I poured myself into books about writing and decorating.

Mr. Blah was in the passenger seat questioning me as I drove home. "Why don't they have a sofa in the bookstore?"

After two weeks of this depression, I decided to ask God for help. (I am a bit slow.) It was hard to pray because it sounded so selfish and silly. I should be the most thankful person on earth, but apparently knowing that and feeling that are two different things. That's the unreasonableness and darkness of depression.

I am not even sure I said, "Dear God." Instead, in my blue mind, I said, "God, what is wrong with me?"

My husband's girls had just left with their two precious babies after dinner one evening. They took my mind off my soul, but the minute they walked away, the Blues brothers put me back on the couch.

I picked up my iPad from the coffee table. I usually write my To Do lists on paper. However, wasn't there a thingy on the iPad for notes? Why should I leave my sofa?

Yes, the note icon!

After opening the app, what I read took my breath away. I must have been on a flight a while back and decided to write. Once I landed, I forgot about it and never hit the icon again. The words read:

"As I fly over the land and rivers below me, I am thankful. I get to see the shape of the earth and soar amid the clouds. I am grateful for the God who blessed little old me to be able to travel by plane or take journeys in my mind.

"I am thankful for the adventures I have had and for those to come. I am grateful for those that have journeyed with me and for those I have not yet met.

"How was I so blessed and others not? Humbled is a big word and it is in that vastness of humbleness I stand. The world is large and this little human so small. I don't deserve any of the things I have. With certainty, I know that they are blessings and gifts from God.

"I wish I could soar beyond the clouds and tell those who

traveled before me, 'thank you.' I would like to go back to those I passed by and stop to hug them.

"However, since I can't, I can only hope they are loved, and my ignorance is forgotten."

God sent my words back to me. A reminder that gratitude and thankfulness for the joys we have, the life we live, and the folks who are a part of it, is the prescription to help rid ourselves of those pesky twins, Blue and Blah.

Am I 100% cured? No, not quite. I am working on it. I notice the Blues brothers are getting grayer and the sofa is getting imprints I don't like to see.

Without a doubt, I have the cure, but I must take my medicine: Heaping tablespoons of Gratitude, a cup of hot Thankfulness Tea, and a big slice of Humble Pie while sitting alone at my table with Dr. God.

"Why Me, Lord?"

Mark Twain said, "The two most important days of your life are the day you are born, and the day you find out WHY?" And, I say, "Amen."

For this old girl, it took me a long time to find the absolute why.

I was six years old and not the healthiest of kids. I remember trying to hide the wheezing from asthma and red eczema that covered my arms and legs. I was always embarrassed when other kids would stare at my arms and hear my coughs, but I just kept plugging along doing the best I could.

One day the teachers assembled all the first and second graders into a line. They were testing for tuberculosis in the school cafeteria. The test didn't hurt very badly even though some of my friends cried.

What hurt was a few days later when they called my name in front of the whole assembly and sent me home. I had reacted to the TB test. Mine was the only name called. I was beyond mortified and scared; kids pointed. I still remember that day as if it just happened.

"Why me, Mama?" I wailed.

"I don't know why, honey," she replied, "but it will be all right."

Many grueling tests followed, but thankfully they showed I didn't have tuberculosis.

When I was fifteen, my father announced we were going to move from our home in Tennessee to Georgia. I was petrified. I remember getting on my knees and begging God to keep us with our friends and near family.

I got on my knees, and said, "Why me, God?"

I remember later as a teen profoundly caring for a boy and can vividly remember how much he did not care for me. There was nothing I could do. The hurt of it caused me to pray many nights, "Why me, Lord?"

There would more broken hearts, a divorce, tough times and an abundance of "why's" throughout my adult life.

I suffered from debilitating clinical depression and found myself at times on the brink of suicide. Thank goodness I cried out for help and received it. Thank goodness I stayed in therapy, but still would often ask, "Why me? Why was I even born? What am I doing here?"

During one of those critical times, I remember my therapist said to me,

"Lynn, I don't worry about you as much as I used to."

"Why?" I was surprised.

"I have learned that no matter how low you get, your faith always pulls you through."

He was right about that. My faith was always my shelter during the storms, and it still is.

I always wondered why I wasn't a private person. I would tell anyone anything. I have always been that way, and it drives my children crazy. I am sorry for that. But, I figure maybe you can help someone else to see they can get through things because you were able to.

And, right there, is the "why."

During my career in Interior Design, I would talk to clients as if they were my best friends. I trusted and loved them.

Once, one of my favorite customers asked me to talk with her daughter who was going through an ordeal similar to one she knew I had experienced.

I did indeed talk to her sweet daughter, and I helped her understand that in life you have to turn sorrow to bravery, heartbreak to faith, and the "whys?" to trust.

All human beings need to discover why they are here. Maybe some are lucky enough to know from the beginning or early in life.

At some point we all have to figure out how some of our most horrible experiences can turn into the best wisdom one can find. Often terrible times reveal the secret of just who we are.

My lungs healed, but they have scars. Asthma left me at age seventeen. Scars are just a mark telling the world you survived. So, I like my scars.

When people have to move, I tell them it could be the best thing in the world. It was for me. Those new friends I met in my new hometown at age fifteen are still some of my best buddies and supporters today.

The young man who did not care for me at all is now my friend. Another that broke my heart is also. How blessed am I?

That is why I write my little stories. That is why I have no fear of doing so. If someone is wondering, "Why me?" Just give it time. The answer will come because each one of us has a purpose.

Each one of us has the drive to live through even the most horrible of storms. Sometimes you think you can't make it, but you can and will. Let God be your shelter and when the sun shines again, take a pocketful of its warmth and spread it to someone who is asking,

"Why me, Lord?"

Finding My Way To The Light After 1988

I was rummaging through an old file labeled "Reflections," and found a poem among the papers. I noticed the date, March 1988, was written on the bottom left corner of the page.

Please, let me go
Let me vanish into a place
Where my spirit will flow
Far away, into a never-ending tomorrow.

I have had enough of trying to try
Laughing when I hurt
Giving and giving
Just more work.

Please, let me die
For I am but a burden
To those who have listened
Only to cry.

I'm only getting worse
May I go?
My life's a curse.

I know you will forgive me
If I interrupt your plan
And let me go by my own hand.

I fought the fight
Now I'm tired
Let me retire
Into your soft night.

Oh, my plans!
You always win
Finding a way to
Give me hope again.

You saved me; heaven knows why
To find purpose, rhyme.
You carried me when I couldn't
Thank you, God,
For loving me
Even when I didn't.

When I read what I wrote in 1988, years slipped away, and I recalled the feeling of being on the inside of depression and darkness. I realized most people only view suicide from the outside looking into the lives of those who see only blackness. The voyeur cannot begin to understand what sorrow lies in the heart of those who take their own lives. The outside world cannot understand those who live where sadness is so profound and those who feel happiness only belongs to others.

When suicide seemed to be the only way to find rest for myself, I believed the world would be a far better place without me. My depressed mind thought my family would be free from my tears and their worry about me, gone. I felt I bothered the world, bothered my family, and I was a bother to myself. I hated being me.

My world was depression, and when God showed me a glimmer of hope, I took it. I worked hard to walk away from the cliff beckoning me to jump, and instead, climbed up the mountain to find life, not death.

I am one of the ones who survived the tomb of the lost. Its

darkness does not discriminate between the young or old, rich or poor. Clinical depression isn't the only reason one can enter the tomb. Situational depression from a tragic loss, physical illness, financial distress, failure, addictions, mental illness, bullying, pressure, resentment, and a myriad of other reasons can place you among the lost.

When we lose a famous person to suicide, we don't quite understand why, when they seemed to live the dream, they would choose death. The truth is they weren't living a dream; they were lost in the nightmare.

Since suicide is on the rise as is mental illness, it is way past the time for us to reveal who we are. It is time to share, to care about each other and be brave enough to talk about our struggles so that others understand they are not alone.

Plus, this idea that mental illness is a stigma or failure is archaic. Everyone needs to trash judgemental thinking because too many are suffering and dying, including our children. Let's love one another and show compassion. Let's stop the whispering and start listening.

If I could be in the same room as the person who is ready to fall off the cliff from life to death, I would grab their arm and tell the story of me.

"There were times in my life I had to fight to keep from jumping off the cliff just like you. Times when loneliness and fatigue multiplied the depression. Times when I worried about money, weariness from jobs, and when sadness followed me around like a shadow. The good news is that I am standing with you now to pull you away from the edge.

"If you fall, you will miss seeing what is awaiting you tomorrow. I found help, I talked, I shared, I prayed, and because I did, I was able to see my children grow into beautiful adults. I saw a precious granddaughter join the world. I fell in love, I continued my career giving it all I could, and when it was over, I started my dream of writing. The bullies will move away, rudeness will be forgotten, and loss will ease with time. So, don't die, let me take you to see the light of tomorrow.

"Tomorrow will turn into weeks and with work, weeks will turn into the future and one that will feel sad if you are not there."

Every single person on this planet is vital and has a reason not to give up. God showed me purpose, gave me a voice and the courage to live long after 1988.

June 2018

Southland

I was born in the hills of East Tennessee, lived in Alabama on two different occasions, and have been a Georgia resident for many years.

The Southland is my home. With my accent and heritage, I doubt other parts of the world would take me. That's fine by me.

To understand the richness found in the South is to realize wealth is not about money. Our fortunes are faith, family, and fried chicken.

The south is where jasmine soothes your soul in spring, and football warms your spirit in winter. We carry a fishing pole in summer months and watch the hills turn amber in fall.

God placed me on Southern soil, and when He did, He blessed me with a patch of heaven.

Dolly, Me, And The Southland

Several years ago, when my granddaughter was six, I decided to take her to Dollywood in Tennessee during her summer visit with me.

We drove from Atlanta through the Great Smoky Mountains winding our way to Pigeon Forge. Once there, we checked into our rooms and then off to the theme park.

The sunny day began to turn dark with clouds. Once the rain started, we quickly made our way to the Dolly Parton Museum where a trio of women warmly greeted us.

"Hello, young lady, what is your name?" one leaned over a counter to ask Avery.

"Well, honey, do you watch Hannah Montana on the TV?" said another.

"Yes ma'am, I do!" Avery responded as her eyes lit up.

"Well, honey child, I am gonna take you upstairs and show you the room where they did some of the filmin'. Sweetheart, you know Miss Dolly played her Grandma on the show, don't you?"

Avery absolutely knew that. During our drive, I had told my grandchild all I knew about Dolly Parton. How we were within fifty miles of one another as children. How Dolly had lived happily with many brothers and sisters in a tiny house in the hills. I explained how her mother made her a coat from scraps of fabric of various colors because they could not afford a store bought one.

As the kind woman showed us the way to the Hannah Montana room, Avery pointed to a glass case, "Grandma! Look! There it is!"

The little coat made of scraps was displayed and lit as if it were a diamond encrusted tiara at a royal museum. Around the bottom of the jacket were pieces of paper where Dolly had scribbled the lyrics to the song that catapulted her to fame.

While we gazed at the "Coat of Many Colors," I was reminded of everything from my grandmother's quilts with their tiny hand sewed stitches, to how, with a dream, rags can become riches.

As we walked through the museum, I continued to tell Avery Dolly stories in hopes that this beautiful, intelligent woman had made a lasting impression on her.

When we exited the building, I asked her what she thought of her experience. "Did you like it, Avery?"

"Yes, I did, but you know what Grandma?"

"What, Avery?"

"Do you know all those people in there talk just like you?!"

I laughed till I cried.

Once you are born and raised in the mountains, the Tennessee accent stays with you. You must attend a particular school to lose it.

I never wanted to because it is a significant part of who I am. When I moved to Georgia as a teen, I remember trying to pick up a bit of the genteel southern accent of my Georgia friends.

I ended up with Chattanooga in accent speak. My interpretation of words never entirely made it across the Georgia line.

I have never been embarrassed about my Southern roots because I love the Southland. I love its people and its diversity plus its endearing charm and charity. I love the way my South Carolinian neighbor says hosepipe instead of hose just like I do. Or a billfold instead of a wallet. And, yes, "Bless Your Heart" is a sentence staple. I love grits, gardens and goin' fishing.

When my son was ten, we moved from Douglasville, Georgia to north of Atlanta, a mere 41 miles away. He was starting

5th grade. Corey never met a stranger, so I wasn't concerned about him making new friends.

During his first teacher conference at his new school, the teacher informed me that Corey was doing ok, but she thought he might be getting bullied because of his accent.

"We are still in the South, aren't we?!" I said slightly sarcastically.

When I returned home, I questioned Corey.

"Oh, mom, it's no big deal, I can handle it" he replied dismissively.

I told him exactly how to handle it anyway.

After a few weeks, I called his teacher to see if there was still a problem.

"No! The teasing ended after I heard Corey telling a group of his friends about his heritage. He told them his southern family had fought in the American Revolution, and his frontiersman ancestors forged the path west. He further stated that if they didn't like the way the South speaks, they should go further north to school!"

The teacher laughed as she told the rest of the story. I beamed with pride, albeit with a slightly red face.

Corey has had those same friends now for 33 years.

Sure, I get teased about my accent. Southerners often are judged by the way we speak. Many try to rid themselves of accents. No one should ever apologize for being and speaking southern. Nor should one should ever apologize for being and speaking northern as well.

I love that this country is made up of regions and differences. It's a lot more fun. If we were all the same, it would get downright dull.

Just like the different scraps of material made a tapestry of warmth and love for a little girl from the hills, the diversity and sounds of our various cultures make up the fabric called "America."

Yes, Dolly Parton's life has changed since she first wore the coat of many colors. Her home now is an impressive mansion. Her intelligence and talents are enormous, yet her accent is still the same.

Thank goodness.

The Magic Of The Fry Pan And Fried Chicken

If you come from the hills of Tennessee or anywhere in the Old South, you probably inherited or own a cast iron skillet. I have a stack of them.

I can still remember my tiny great-grandmother standing over her wood burning stove, apron tied around her waist, hair twisted in a bun, cooking something in her old, black fry pan.

My grandmother had the skillet next, along with an assortment of other sizes that were handed down to her or she bought. One day right before I married, she handed it to me, so now I own that skillet. It is at least 150 years old and still frying.

Grandpa was the funniest woman I ever knew. I still remember her hoisting that heavy cast iron fry pan over her head by the handle saying, "Now, Lynn, you know you can use this for things other than frying, don't you? Don't you let anyone hurt you! You whack 'um with this if they do, you hear?"

When I lived alone for many years, I had that heavy iron skillet under the bed. I would take it out only when I needed to fry up some magic.

My mother, the next one in line, swore you couldn't eat a better grilled cheese than one she fried in butter using her little iron skillet. She was right; you couldn't. The tiny black pan holds only one sandwich and will bake just enough cornbread for two.

Every time I cook using one of these skillets, the memories return of the beautiful, strong, southern women who used them. I am so blessed to call them "family."

I have determined that fried chicken is as magical as my

pans.

I learned to fry it years ago. My recipe is unusual and comes from someone else's grandma in Florida. I'll bet they used an old iron skillet that has its own batch of stories.

When you have an accent like mine, folks expect you to know how to cook fried chicken. That's the truth!

My friend, Susan, was diagnosed with incurable cancer many years ago at the age of 52. She went through brutal rounds of chemotherapy. During that time, the nausea was so severe it was hard for patients to eat anything during their treatment.

I was with her when the doctor told her she had to eat. He put her on milkshakes and eggs. She hated both. I looked at her and declared, "No Susan, you need your favorite meal: My fried chicken and green beans!"

When I returned home, I pulled my iron skillet from under the bed and fried her a batch of chicken. Once I arrived at her house, she ate several pieces along with those fresh green beans. She never got sick.

I accompanied her again to the doctor the next week. He asked her if she had been able to eat anything.

"Yes, fried chicken and green beans!" she beamed.

Astounded and perplexed, the doctor was silent.

I intervened, "Doc, don't you know southern fried chicken is healing and the fry pan, magical?"

My chicken didn't cure Susan, of course, but it sure did heal her spirit for a while.

How many times have friends gathered around my table drooling over crispy fried chicken? Even those who eat only green and those who never eat anything golden, suddenly are devouring the word "never."

The other day I had lunch with an old, dear friend. He has struggled this past year with illness and is not entirely out of the woods.

However, I am sure he will be because he is the tallest, best tree in the forest and there are endless amounts of people praying for him.

I thought he knew most things about me, but as we were dining, the conversation drifted to fried chicken. I told him about my stack of fry pans and my specialty.

"You fry chicken?!" He was shocked.

When I told him I had done so for years and about the chicken's magical properties, his eyes lit up and his mouth watered. How the heck had we known each other for so long without his knowing that tidbit of information I'll never know! We both laughed as I promised him a plate soon.

It's funny about the little things in life. How something as seemingly small as an old fry pan and a piece of southern fried chicken can evoke special memories, cure illness for a moment, gather friends around a table, and give a promise to a special pal who stands tall in the forest.

That kind of magic is a beautiful, golden thing.

Southern Belles And Steel Magnolias

Now and then in life, you meet a real Southern Belle who is also a Steel Magnolia. My family consisted of many Belles who grew into steel rods who supported an entire family while keeping their genteel nature. Those women paved the way for all of us to understand grit, determination, and bravery. Learning from their valuable lives gives us a real education into what courage means.

Geri lives down the street. Several years ago, she was preparing for an operation on her foot. Before surgery, the doctor ordered a routine chest x-ray which saved her life.

She didn't have foot surgery, but lung surgery. The cancer was caught just in time to avoid chemo and other harsh treatments. It took her a while to get her stamina back, but soon Geri was well and thriving.

Geri was born in south Alabama. She is a tall, beautiful woman who raised two daughters, mostly alone. She had to work two jobs to support her little family. After Geri divorced the children's father, she remarried for a short time once her girls were adults. On a Sunday while watching television, her newlywed husband lay his head in her lap for a nap and never woke up.

His death was devastating and sudden. Again, Geri had to find the grit to overcome the sorrow. The Southern Belle fought to gain strength and determination to laugh again. Time passed. She eventually met and married Tom.

Two years ago, Tom began feeling ill. He just couldn't shake what he thought was bronchitis. Tom, a never-smoker, would soon learn he also had lung cancer.

The situation was dire until a new drug worked miracles! Tom and Geri soon started taking trips, laughing, and enjoying life down the street.

Geri was born on St. Patrick's Day. Supposedly the luck of the Irish was to smile upon her. However, on March 17, 2017, the leprechaun didn't visit the house down the street.

Geri has taken care of her 100-year-old mother for as long as I have known her and never complains. When folks are sick, she is there with one of her signature Southern dishes that make your mouth water. When she entertains, it is over the top. But, what else would you expect from a real Southern Belle?

At parties, her laughter rises above the room, letting you know that she is there and in force. She uses the "Bless Your Heart" ending in sentences just like I do and still loves things made from scratch.

Another couple, along with my husband and me, were at a local restaurant for St. Patrick's Day. We all saw Tom and Geri plus a guest visiting them, heading toward our table to say hello. They were celebrating Geri's birthday.

We all wished her birthday blessings and laughed. She looked elegant and relaxed with her warm smile highlighting her face. You would have never guessed earlier that same day her doctor had called to tell her the devastating news that a different type of cancer was now in her right lung.

When I thought about how cheerful she was, how gracious she was amidst learning the horrific news, my first thought was, "What a Steel Magnolia!"

I believe I am strong, but I don't hold a candle to this steel rod of strength. When she sent a text to her friends telling them about this new-found illness, various people immediately texted back. One of our mutual friends was on vacation and sent words of prayer and encouragement.

Geri's response, "I have turned everything over to God. It is out of my hands. Hope you are enjoying your vacation! Have fun and relax!"

Steel Magnolias know from where their strength comes. They know who can help them stand when life knocks them down. The Southern Belle knows to try not to worry others. She is still thinking of her friends and family even though her world could be crumbling.

So many folks stroll through life with the attitude, "Why me?" They wear it proudly as a symbol of their doomsday take on life. And then there is Geri. Her smile takes away the doom, her strength takes away sadness, and her Steel Magnolia theory teaches us all about real courage.

After learning her diagnosis on her birthday, I figure she is planning for her treatments, calming her family, and will probably make a homemade pie by the end of the day. After brushing her blond hair, she will apply her makeup and check on her mother. She will worry about the neighbor down the street and a grandchild going to college.

The Belles dance in their elegant dresses and perfectly coifed hair; they appear delicate as a flower. They dance with their beaus and remember the family that taught them the steps of the dance.

At some point during the ball, the Belle danced with God himself who turned the delicate flower into a beautiful Steel Magnolia.

Spring Has Sprung In Georgia

The azaleas are bursting into shades of bright pinks and corals against a backdrop of spring green. Dogwoods are blossoming using their delicate ivory petals to tell the story of Christ. New buds are patiently waiting to paint dull gray tree branches into vibrancy. Pollen is sprinkling fine yellow dust on cars, porches, houses, and making its way into sinus cavities everywhere.

Yes, spring has sprung in Georgia.

Chipmunks are awake, birds are singing, and life is in renew mode. Kids see the end of another school year approaching and can feel the summer sun just around the bend. Graduations in May, weddings in June, and vacations are waiting in the wings.

Yes, spring has sprung in Georgia.

When I glance in my closet, I see only grays, blacks, and charcoals paired with blue jeans. It is beyond drab and so wintery I notice a snowflake falling on the Christmas sweater. Maybe I should plant a pink azalea under the racks or perhaps go shopping. My husband votes for the azalea idea.

Yes, spring has sprung everywhere in Georgia except for my closet.

Did we not just celebrate Christmas? Did I miss a few months of living? Why does the clock need springing forward when I just sprang it back a few days ago?

This not-so-spring chicken has a hard time keeping up with all the renewed springing happening around me!

The seasons are starting to come a little too fast for me now. Days fly by, and I want to grab each one and hold onto its moments as if they were as precious as diamonds.

The Masters golf tournament is this week in Augusta. I was born into the world of golf. My father was likely on a golf course somewhere with Bobby Jones when mom delivered me. Perhaps it is the Scottish DNA which propelled Dad to shine his golf shoes and mom to iron her Bermuda shorts when the spring air started to float down the fairways, and a warm breeze swayed the pines.

Every time I watch the tournament in April, my mind recalls the parents who waited for the spring day when they could witness Arnold Palmer, Sam Snead, or Ben Hogan hit the famed links at Augusta.

On the wall near my desk is a framed photograph of three children all dressed in Sunday finery posed for the camera. Amy, the eldest, is nine with a slight smile curved upward as curls frame her sweet face. Tiny Heather is six and happily unaware that her big smile shows off a mouth with very few teeth. Corey, with his grin and impish face, is age four wearing a suit with lapels so wide they touch each shoulder. It is Easter day 1979.

My three little children are now all grown, and my parents are hopefully watching their old golf heroes play on the heavenly links above the clouds in the Master's realm.

Yet, today spring is still being sprung in Georgia just as it did all those years ago. The same old oak with its bud-filled branches falls over the same patch of earth providing shade from the Georgia heat for another generation.

I believe God sends us spring to remind us that hope is just under the surface of all things in life. And, as sure as I say I can't keep up with it all, He is going to spring another season on me anyway. Life moves on whether we are ready for it or not and that is as it should be.

The blessing of spring and all the beauty and joy it brings teaches us that we can renew our hearts anytime. We can become more vibrant if we want to. We can wake up smiling with Mother Nature on a spring morn, or we can hide under the covers, wait for winter, and miss the whole dang thing.

Personally, I will plant my azalea in my closet, dust off the pollen from the table tops, take Sudafed and watch the old oak sprout leaves. I plan on finding something new about myself daily until the day I play golf again with my parents.

I will not mourn my youth, nor the springs gone by but instead rejoice in the memories of the seasons I have witnessed and happily attempt to grab those that are flying by me now.

Just as sure as the sun rises and falls, spring comes to Georgia with all its heavenly glory telling us to renew our lives, our spirits, and reminding us to always to continue to grow.

It's All About The Ride

I decided to drive to Ft. Lauderdale the other day instead of flying. My granddaughter was graduating from elementary school. I try to miss nothing when it comes to her. However, this story is not about the most precious thing in the world; it's about the ride.

Flying to Ft. Lauderdale from Atlanta takes two hours. Driving there takes ten. That is why I usually fly Delta. However, I needed to take my children some furniture they wanted. I thought this trip would provide a good opportunity, but I had dreaded the long drive for days.

I-75 South is, how do I say, not the most scenic route in America. Then top that off with the Florida Turnpike and the word "boring" takes on even more monotony!

The sun was just barely over the horizon when I pulled out of my driveway looking like Ma Clampett heading to Beverly Hills. Furniture was stacked in the back of the SUV with bungee cords holding it tight and clothes were thrown in bags in between.

I had not yet closed the car window when the smell of Confederate Jasmine seeped in. I smiled and looked at the vines in full bloom scenting the air with their sweet aroma. I noticed the beads of water on the grass and the green of the trees bursting with beautiful new growth.

"Wow, I sure wish my drive could look like this!" I said to myself as I drove away.

Traffic was light to my great surprise, and before I knew it, I was heading toward Macon, Georgia. I would stop there briefly.

After filling up on coffee and gas, I continued my journey. I turned the radio to the 60s station and listened to the music I know well. Songs evoke the strangest feelings if you let them. I remembered my friends from high school and college. Why do you always miss your old classmates? You just do.

The road became flat and straight, so I started reading the billboards that line the highway. You can have the world's most fabulous meal at Papa Somebodies for $5. Then came Cordele, "The Gateway to South Georgia." There is Jolly RV park, Antique Malls with thousands of square feet, and a King Frog Clothing store beckoning you. Some signs made me laugh out loud.

There is something for every traveler on this road. How could one be bored?

When I reached Valdosta, Georgia, I sent a message to a friend that calls this his hometown.

"I am waving to you as I pass through to Florida!" I guess my friend thought that silly, but I refused not to be entertained.

The sun was shining as I decided to start looking beyond the billboards to the hill-less land of south Georgia. My son was born in Moultrie where I lived for only a year. I loved Moultrie, and those south Georgia bugs didn't bother much because I had excellent friends there who never bugged me.

I passed vibrant green pastures where cows grazed and lay among shade trees. Farmland was abundant with new crops, and an occasional tractor sighting made me think of my Granddaddy.

Finally, I crossed the Florida Line. New billboards were advertising Disney Discount Tickets. A rest area and Welcome Station were coming up. Had to stop. I watched kids getting their picture taken in front of a molded 5-foot-tall dolphin statue. Their father, trying to get them back in the car.

"Come on guys. Mickey Mouse is waiting for us!" That did it; they headed toward the waiting car.

Gosh, I remember my first trip to Disney with my kids. How

inventive was old Walt for building a park that would delight so many children? He was a genius indeed.

The world's most giant alligator was just a mile ahead along with the free orange juice. I remember seeing that gator with my parents on the first vacation we ever took. We rode in a hot, un-air-conditioned car for twelve hours and I wouldn't take anything for it.

The next thing I knew I was on the double dull Florida Turnpike and the Beach Boys were playing summer songs. How I always loved the beginning of summer.

Every June I thought, "Whew, I made it through another school year!" Vacation, visiting my grandparents, swimming, sleeping late. I loved catching those lightning bugs, watching fireworks, and watermelon feasts. Picnics and hayrides were a special treat.

"Oops, my exit is here! How did that happen so fast? My back doesn't even hurt!"

The following morning at 9 a.m., I watched my most precious thing in the world graduate to middle school with honors. I was very proud.

However, I needed to be sure to tell her something when we got back to her house:

"Avery, life is not about the destination but more about taking the time to enjoy the journey. Take time to smell the jasmine, listen to an old song and often think about wonderful friends and family. Take the opportunity to laugh at silly stuff, and learn from any mistakes you make. Keep your eyes focused on the God that turns the pastures green and provides a shade tree for all of us. Remember it is an honor to take the ride. If you do, the journey will never be boring, but instead, downright beautiful."

Just like my drive.

Healing

There are occasions in our lives when our heart seems to stop, and fear replaces the air. Times when illness or an accident creeps into our existence threatening to take our lives away.

These are the days when our frailty falls into the hands of physicians, nurses, family, friends, and God. These are the moments when we must try to replace tears with hope and pain with courage.

It is during our weakest days that we often find our inner strength and attitude will move us into the grace of healing.

Forever In Pink

Most everyone knows that October is Breast Cancer Awareness Month. If you are not aware, you must not get out much. Pink ribbons are everywhere. Even NFL players wear some form of pink during every October game. Pink trinkets entice you to buy them in every shop.

Yes, October and pink are as synonymous as October and Halloween.

However, the House of Pink is a place that, once you enter, your understanding of what pink represents will be forever altered. Once you have walked through the pink door, you no longer just pass the trinkets, or just notice the pink gloves on the football players, or just tie a pink ribbon in a child's hair; you will now notice the color pink with a chill creeping up your spine. And, the chill never goes away.

My grandmother loved the color pink. It was her absolute favorite. It became mine as well. I never was sure if I liked the color or just loved her. It didn't matter; up until 2011, pink still was my favorite color because it reminded me of my favorite person.

Admission to the pink house is always shocking. Whether it is your own diagnosis of breast cancer, or a diagnosis in someone you love, it knocks your world upside down.

For me, breast cancer happened to someone I loved: my daughter. She and I held on tight the first day we walked into pink. A world of testing, medical terminology, oncology, surgeons, geneticists, MRIs, glaring lights, and fear.

You have no time to prepare for your stay in the pink world because it consumes you immediately. You must dig deep into your soul to places you never knew existed to find the courage to keep walking and breathing. All you have is the love of each other and faith to keep you moving inside this new, scary place. There is no escape.

During the months our family spent in the halls of the pink home, the outside world seemed far away. Time and space appeared altered. People we never knew before became strong allies and friends. People we did know became lightning rods of support and hope. God became more visible and unquestionable.

Hope covers the walls in the pink house. Hope is the main ingredient served at every meal, and it fortifies you. Every day is a walk to tomorrow with crutches made of faith and stumbles caused by fear. Every day we pleaded with God and doctors. Every day turns into a night of tossing and doubting.

Mirrors in the pink world's chambers reflect beautiful heads with no strands of beautiful hair. Circles are under sad eyes filled with tears or sickness. But the reflection also shows a group standing behind you.

They whisper, "You will return, your hair will grow, your circles will fade." They are the sisterhood that once walked the halls in the pink house. Without them, this pink world would turn to solid gray gloom.

Once you are a patient in the middle of the journey in this rosy world, you will have calmed a bit and accepted the fight you are in. You draw your swords as you tackle the pain and illness running through your body which now has become almost foreign to you.

You allow harsh chemicals to enter a port in your chest to kill cells within you. You sit and worry about what the effects of these will do to you both now and later, while the rest of your brain is reading a magazine. You have no choice. Your choices are now gone. Cancer took them away.

Then one day you catch a glimpse of the green of the trees, the blue of the sky, the brown of the earth. The pink is starting to fade. The hair begins to return, and the scars begin to heal. The nights become bearable, and food starts to have flavor again. You realize, with awe, you have lived for a year in the pink world.

It has now been six years since Heather and our family left the pink house. As I look back, I can still see it filled with others who have just entered and those who are getting ready to go. Its rosy hue is always transforming the gloomy old house to a brighter, more hopeful one.

Heather and I know the rear door of the house stays open. You learn to live with the knowledge that you will always be a card-carrying member of the sorority of pink. It is the sisterhood that allows you to do so.

Yes, pink still is my favorite color. I loved the grandmother who wore pink, but I adore the daughter who lived it. Both were and are the finest and bravest women I will ever know.

Next time you pass a pink ribbon, or a pink trinket, or watch an NFL player wearing pink shoes, remember these things are there to remind you of a world you or someone you love could enter at any moment.

I hope you never enter that house, but if you do, I can guarantee the survivors who are forever in pink will hold your hand throughout the journey and God will give you the swords for the battle.

The Miracle In The Sun

There are a few of you who may have doubts that miracles occur. I think they happen every day. We are often so consumed with our intelligence that cynical blindness clouds miracles from God.

It was a beautiful September day in 2014 in Gulf Shores, Alabama. A morning where the sun glistens on the ocean and the sounds of waves kissing the shore soothe your soul.

Our family vacation was just beginning. All fifteen of us were looking forward to seven days of laughter and fun. We are boisterous group of folks who love one another. However, from the very start of this day, I felt out of sorts.

It was the day we were renting the big pontoon boat in order to spend all day on the water at Perdido Key Bay. Everyone was excited, except me; dread filled my heart for no apparent reason.

Midafternoon, we pulled the boat onto a tiny strip of land with a sandy beach surrounded by warm, shallow water. Everyone jumped into the water as I tried to relax on the boat.

My back was turned away from the scene of activity when I felt a hand touch my arm from the water below.

"Mom," Corey whispered, "I think I've hurt myself."

My 39-year-old son looked noticeably gray.

"What did you do?" I questioned.

"I dove into the water and hit my head on the sand. I think I hurt my shoulder; it feels funny."

I noticed his normal rosy cheek color was now ashen and a sense of urgency swelled in my soul. I tried to hurry everyone to return to the boat. I felt we must make sure my son was not badly injured.

Everyone filed on board not understanding the gravity both Corey and I felt. Corey was sitting near the end of the pontoon and once everyone was seated he jumped off the boat and single-handedly pushed it off the sand with all the might he could muster while ignoring my yells for him to stop.

Once he was back on the boat with his girlfriend, Kendra, I watched him as he jerked his neck left then right as if to pop it. Without warning, tears started to cascade down my cheeks.

The closest trauma hospital was Sacred Heart in Pensacola. It was the opposite direction of where our rented vacation home was in Gulf Shores. We decided that all should return to the house except my daughter Heather, who would drive Kendra, Corey, and me to the hospital so Corey could be examined.

The traffic lined the two-lane road creating delays and time was of the essence.

Just as we see the hospital, Corey quietly said, "I think we need to hurry." While he had tried to protect us from worry, he finally gave in to the gravity of the situation.

Panic and fear filled my body. Life was happening in lightning bolts and giant waves. My heart was pounding, my daughter pale, Kendra scared.

After a few minutes in the crowded waiting area, we were called into one of three cubicles to give pertinent information to a young woman. As Corey was telling her what happened, a man appeared in the empty cubicle behind us. He was the head nurse in ER and happened to need a form at the exact moment Corey was explaining his accident.

"You know what, let me see if I can expedite you to x-ray. Sit in this wheelchair and try not to move until I see if it's available," he emphatically stated.

"On second thought," the nurse added, 'let me just take you with me."

The staff escorted Kendra, Heather, and me to an ER room. Corey returned and was joking with the nurse. He was flat on a gurney now with a hard neck brace supporting him.

A woman entered the room, smiled broadly, and introduced herself as the ER physician. She examined Corey while waiting for the scan results.

Toes wiggled perfectly; strength perfect, sensation perfect, and hands moved fluently. "Corey, you look good, but let's stay still until we get those results."

I felt more comfortable now that she had indicated that he would be fine.

After a few minutes, she walked back into the room. Her demeanor had noticeably changed. Fear immediately overwhelmed me.

"Mr. Lockman, you have an angel on your shoulder. You do have a broken neck. I have never seen an injury like this with the spinal cord still intact." The doctor was shaking her head in disbelief.

Upon hearing this, I left the room, walked to a corner and beat my fist into the walls. For a minute, I went into a dark hole that consumed me. I became utterly overcome with self-pity. My daughter saw my distress and grabbed me while teams of doctors raced into the tiny ER room and tended to my only son.

Then God came walking down the hall. I felt Him as he filled me with courage, conviction, and trust. I climbed out of the dark hole as fast as I fell into it. I returned to the room and realized I was alone with Corey. The room was dimly lit and eerily quiet. It was as if we were suspended in time, a break in activity, a moment to be mother and son.

I held his hand as tears slid down his cheeks. Surgery was going to take place; a metal plate, screws, and danger.

"Mom, I need to tell you some important information. I don't have much in life, but I do have a couple of insurance policies, and you are the beneficiary. Please save the money to give to my niece to help finance her education." He also told me his wishes if he did not survive.

"Mom, pray with me." I took both of his hands and prayed

for God's will and help. Just as I finished a long prayer, the lights brightened, and people again were in a flurry of activity around my son. Where had they all gone? Odd.

Once in ICU, teams of folks including doctors, chaplains, nurses, and students would look in to see the miracle of Corey. There was no paralysis, no side effects from the broken neck that he had twisted and turned for many hours after the initial fracture.

As the months passed and we all resumed life, both Corey and I wondered many "why's?" We saw so many with the same injury left with quadriplegia, confined to wheelchairs. Why was Corey spared?

All I can tell you for sure is that a miracle occurred on that sunny day. The miracle affected many. It touched those who were not too blind to see that God carried my son to safety from a place where the water meets the sky in heavenly shades of azure blue.

The Visit To The ER

There must be a law written somewhere that if one goes into labor, gets very sick, or needs a doctor in a hurry for any reason, it will be late in the evening or the wee hours of the morning. To add insult to injury, many times those events occur on the weekend.

Yes, I think there is a law written somewhere.

Of course, on a Friday night about ten p.m., I had to go for one of those visits to the Emergency Room. Of course, my husband was out of town. Of course, the pharmacy had closed, and of course, it was the start of the weekend.

I am fine now, but an infection went awry, of course, at an inopportune time!

My friend and neighbor, Deborah, took me. Bless her sweet heart! It helps to live next door to an angel. I don't enjoy bothering my angels or anyone else's for that matter.

Of course, waiting for me was a crowded waiting room. Hospitals couldn't have called a "Waiting Room" a better name because "wait" is all you do.

After I gave my intake information to the kind lady in the reception area, a nurse took my vitals and drew blood. She returned a few moments later to insert an IV in my left arm and then sent me back to my chair to wait beside Deborah.

"Why the IV?" Deborah asked.

"Not sure, but it sure makes me look as if I officially belong here," I replied with a chuckle.

When I glanced around noticing the others waiting, I realized I could write an entire book about the folks in the ER.

A woman was so ill that she was lying on her husband's lap as he stroked her back. Her color was just short of white, and her pain was evident in the sad eyes resembling gray pools above her white mask.

Deborah and I hoped she would see a doctor soon. I was in pain but was not as sick as she was. I could wait.

A little boy sat across from us. His huge brown eyes were continually searching for someone or something to calm his fear. His dad, or a male in his life, was asleep in the chair beside him. His mother, silent, was holding on to her slightly swollen abdomen. It was hard to discern which one was needing an emergency room.

We deduced the mother might be pregnant and in trouble. I looked for an ID band on her wrists. There it was, the band which put pure fear in her son's eyes.

It was after midnight when the nurse escorted the boy's mother to a room for evaluation. The accompanying man was still asleep in the chair. The child, with wide-open eyes, continued to stare at the door waiting for his mother.

We hoped that she would return to the waiting room with good news. We prayed for love to replace fear in a little boy with big brown eyes. He needed it and, again, I could wait.

Around 1 a.m., an elderly gentleman strolled in holding on to a cane. He was alone. I glanced several times at the door, looking for anyone who might have accompanied him. No one ever came.

His loneliness overwhelmed me. Where was the angel neighbor or the family? There was none.

"I could wait. The pain has eased," I convinced myself.

"Cancel code blue, cancel code blue!" the voice from the intercom repeated.

"Wonder who that was for?" I asked Deborah as if she would know.

"I hope it wasn't for that sick woman who had been waiting for so long," Deborah responded.

We sat silent for a moment thinking about how precarious living can be. How within just moments, a code blue could be for you or someone you love.

"Lynn Gendusa?" I heard someone call in the background.

I rose, and Deborah followed.

A young, cute waif of a female doctor met me beside the massive wooden doors leading to the exam rooms.

"You have a nasty infection, but we have no ER rooms left. It has been a crazy night, so I decided to put you in this triage area to examine you," she apologetically explained as she led the way.

Deborah sat on the gurney beside me. The IV came in handy for the big dose of the antibiotics I needed, plus some fluid.

The young ER doctor couldn't have been more helpful. The accompanying nurses were worn and frazzled by the stream of patients with various illnesses who had walked through their doors.

All the medical staff was staying on past their shifts to help out on this busy Friday night in January.

I tried to keep them laughing to lift their spirits and mine.

How many times do we take those that heal us for granted?

How many times have we thought our pain was more intense than that of others and that we deserved to be first because of it?

How mad do we get because we are forced to wait?

How sobering it is to realize that others need help before we do. How grateful we are when an intercom voice cancels a "Code blue," or a little boy returns to his mother's arms.

"Thank you!" I said with sincerity as I left, but for some reason, two words just didn't seem enough.

Deborah and I left for home a little after 2 a.m. in the morning. Yes, I was still uncomfortable, but as strange as it sounds, I am not sure I will ever see the ER quite the same again.

I saw it as a place for others to get help and healing.

For me, I could wait.

Maybe I grew up a bit when I learned I needed to follow the law "It's Not All About Me."

The Second We Fall Into Everlasting Arms

A text message lit my cell phone screen. After reading the first sentence, a chill crept down my spine. Seconds before, I had been enjoying a pleasant drive home to Atlanta from south Florida. Old tunes played on the radio while the sun warmed the car. Old tunes that reminded me of sock hops and school days. Happy that traffic was light, and that my spirit was in a joyful, quiet place.

Then the message. An old high school friend had fallen on a black diamond ski slope in Nevada. An avid, trained, excellent skier who was accustomed to such treacherous runs, became motionless in the snow. Severely injured, he then was airlifted to a trauma center in Reno. In less than a minute, this fit, robust man who could fly down the highest slopes was now flying away to be saved by teams of doctors.

In less than a minute, my warm spirit moved into the cold chill of tragedy. In less than a minute, the skies that had been sunny were now gray, and rain had started to fall. "How apropos," I thought.

How many times in our lives have we been gliding through a day, breezily thinking of the mundane only to have it upended by a terrible message? How many times in our lives does sunshine turn to storms in a second?

The longer we live, the more we experience life-changing turns of reality. These can be challenging and horrific. When a disaster occurs, we may think we will not survive to see another sunny day. Whether these tragedies are mental, physical, or spiritual, they test our resolve and resilience.

I am in awe of the strength that can arise from such downfalls. I am always amazed at the power of our inner being. How can we go from wondering what we are going to have for dinner, to facing death, or illness, or a fall down a black diamond in a less than a minute?

I believe this aiding power is not ours at all. The strength that fills us in those horrible times is the power of God. If you can't see him there, you probably need new glasses. It is that power which shines through the darkness of tragedy and serves as a beacon to guide us back into the light of day.

I will never forget another friend standing in a church, giving a eulogy for his son who had tragically, suddenly died. The beacon of strength that shone through him that day was an inspiration to all who witnessed it. I immediately thought, "If he can stand and do this, then his strength will inspire me to face anything."

Have you ever met folks who complain about stupid stuff? I sure have. They worry about everything and obsess about things that don't matter. They hold onto to resentment and anger as if these are valuable traits. "Have these folks ever lived through a tragedy?" I wonder.

For if they had, they didn't get the message that each second counts. They didn't quite get the fact that when we travel through tribulation, we can pick up more faith, wisdom, and thankfulness to aid us in our travels on down the road.

The real tragedy occurs when we don't embrace life and make our seconds count on this earth. When we put things off, when we don't call a friend in need, when we don't take care of ourselves, when we don't try, and when we don't forgive, we are not living life to the fullest. When we don't understand that loves can be lost, and lives can change in a matter of a second, we cannot appreciate the seconds we have.

Have you ever met folks who were afraid to try something new or different because they were afraid of failing, falling, or dying? I sure have. Fear of failure, falling or dying is a sure way to avoid the freedom found in living.

Yes, my high school friend suffered a tragic ski accident. But how many times did he enjoy the ski runs? How many times did he feel the wind fly by as he swished through the pristine white powder?

After the bones heal, and the rehab is over, my pal will once again glide across the glistening snow. The storm will have passed. The sun will warm the air as he fills his mind with old tunes, family, good friends, and thankfulness.

Our world can turn in a second, but when we lean on the healing power of God's everlasting arms, soon the seconds will turn into hours, days, and the rest of our lives.

Age(less)

When I was young, someone once said to me, "Lynn, you are an old soul."

Well, I believe my age has now caught up with my soul!

To turn a year older is a gift and should be celebrated with family, friends, cake and if lucky, enough candles to burn down the house. I appreciate I have been given the opportunity to age, but I will do my best to keep my spirit young.

Each year that passes is a chance to learn more, love more, and recognize the beauty of each given day.

Happy Birthday To You

A **friend of mine** is turning seventy this week. Matter of fact, I know hundreds of folks who will turn seventy this year, including me.

In 1947, the year of my birth, soldiers were returning home from a war that ravaged the world. Open arms, big dreams, and great celebration awaited them. Soon afterward began a boom in the bundles of joy arriving to American homes.

The generation of Baby Boomers born between 1946 and 1955 is bound together by the sights and sounds we have witnessed simultaneously. On Saturday mornings we watched "Howdy Doody," "Sky King," and "Mighty Mouse" on the new device called the TV. On Sunday, we ate fried chicken or pot roast after church. On Monday, we met at school where we laughed and learned together.

In 1962 when President Kennedy died, we held our hands and prayed. We mourned together when we lost a friend or brother during our years in Viet Nam. We applauded when we witnessed the first man to orbit the earth, and by the time we left for college, segregation was soon to be history.

We danced to the beat of the Supremes and sang along with the Beatles, Elvis, and Marvin Gaye playing on our radios. Together we started driving our cars, driving our parents crazy, and driving ourselves into the future.

When I thought of my friend turning seventy, it made me realize how special turning older is. I understand that age is just a number attached to us by a paper calendar.

My friend, along with countless others, really hasn't aged at all. Age is in the spirit, in the heart, and in looking into the deeper meaning of life. The worst mistake seventy-year-olds make is to think of themselves as seventy.

I thought about my brother who only lived to be 56. My friend, Krista, died at 52, sadly before she had the opportunity to hold a grandchild. A young man I adored lived to be fourteen and another to 31. Countless folks we know and love never were able to see the bright side of age. However, their short lives make me more appreciative of my time here and the folks that fill my time.

If I had been born twenty years later or more, I wouldn't have been able to have the friends, loves, and family that I do. I wouldn't have been able to watch my class of '65 win a state basketball championship or drive my friends miles in my 1962 Ford to get Krispy Kremes.

Being born in 1947 and turning seventy is good for me. I love the things I do, and I appreciate the blessings I have. I still have the same crazy spirit, I still talk too much, I always overthink, and I still love Krispy Kremes.

I have climbed over a mountain to a place where what other people think of me is not as important as what I think of myself. I have climbed down to where I can see God's face a little clearer. I can look back at my journey and realize, with gratefulness, He was holding my hand the entire way.

Like all those born in our generation, we have reached or passed the pinnacle of our careers. We realize it wasn't our careers that made us successful, but how well we did our jobs, whatever they may have been.

We must understand that we now can pass wisdom to those who will one day turn seventy if they are so lucky.

Often our children think of us as archaic, rolling their eyes when we can't text as rapidly as they can, or even find the phone, for that matter. However, when they need advice they still call. When they can't find their way or need a recipe, they again turn to us to get directions.

Those same children, grandchildren, friends and family are

the lights that illuminated the way on our journey to seventy and beyond.

With a twinkle in her eye, my mother said to me right before she died, "Lynn, are you ever going to grow up?"

"I haven't planned on it, Mom!" We both laughed.

I don't dread my September birthday. I realize I have walked some beautiful shores, been welcomed with hugs, fulfilled some dreams and have experienced great joy.

To my friend who's turning seventy, and to all of you who are blessed to add another year of living, celebrate your birthday with unbridled joy. Life is beautiful, and every day that you live a bit longer, you realize just how special it is.

And finally, don't look in the mirror, because it lies...Just like that calendar.

Irma, Birthdays, And Dog Hair

Hurricane Irma blew my children from the east coast of Florida to my house in Atlanta two weeks ago. Three adults, one child, a tiny white dog, and a horse/dog named Bodhi, spent exhausting hours in a car to reach the safety of our home.

Today the house is quiet, since all have returned to Florida to find normalcy among fallen trees, flickering power, and roads strewn with sand.

Along with the silence, what's left in Atlanta is a house filled with dog hair, sheets that require changing, towels that need folding, games that need putting away and a refrigerator that, I swear, Irma herself whirled through.

Irma coincided with my birthday trip. My birthday isn't until the end of the month, but it seemed that the weekend of September 15 was chosen to accommodate us all. Irma, however, changed those plans, causing everyone to arrive early!

Yes, I have lived six decades. I thought turning seventy was going to be tough. Decade-changing birthdays are usually traumatic and eventful, so it's good they typically bring family and friends together to help you blow out all those candles.

The weekend of September 15 was full of wonderful surprises, visiting relatives, friends, and stories told with abundant laughter. As I looked at those I love, I realized turning seventy is just about the best age possible.

To make it to seventy is a great reason to rate it best. My brother never did, nor did my friend Krista, nor did Sharon who died in an accident after graduating from high school. We always want more money and years, but some never have a chance to accumulate either.

While I was watching my family across the table and friends laughing at some of my crazy antics, I realized life boils down to being appreciative of the people who've made my seventy years special ones. Those folks are the ones who held my hand and supported my dreams. They gave me the opportunity to feel deep love and be humbled by it.

I have made many errors in past decades. However, they are a part of who I am today. My mistakes made me empathetic to others and taught me forgiveness is way better than resentment.

I accept there are people whom I once loved that I will never see again on this earth. However, it's ok because I was blessed to know them.

There were heartaches and sadness on my road to seventy, but what joy it was to take the ride and survive the crashes along the way. They made me strong and brave. I now write about them, which is quite amazing. My guess is that was not by accident as well.

When I turned six, Mama made me a dark chocolate cake with pink icing for my birthday. I hated frosting, but just wanted to see the pink. I got a kitten that year who I named Sparky. I was allergic to Sparky but loved him too much to give him away. I sneezed and itched for many years. I learned at six that when you love something, there are sacrifices you always must make. That allergy was the sacrifice I made for Sparky and he was worth it. I also ate Mama's icing that day for the same reason.

When I was in high school, I was insecure about my looks and my personality. Matter of fact, I was uncertain about everything. I wanted to be anyone but me. As I aged, I came to understand that God molded me for a reason: to be who I am. I learned to be secure by looking not at me, but at Him.

This weekend amid the clutter, the dogs licked my hands, my children told me I was loved, my friends accepted me as I am and helped me blow out all those candles. What else could one want in life?

Today I will sweep up the dog hair, pack up the games on the table, and take Irma out of the fridge. I now have the wisdom to know that even those things provide precious memories and turning seventy might just be the pink icing on the cake.

These Old Hands

I was in design school with only an hour for lunch. Veronica and I shared classes, and we were starving. We ran down the street to a crowded, student-filled café.

While sitting across from Veronica, I observed her. I was always in awe of her grace and elegance. Raven hair curled down to her shoulders. Perfectly fit designer clothes hugged her slim body that was also perfect. Her manicured hands were gracefully gesturing, and her posture was, of course, impeccable. If there was anyone that ever looked the part of an "Interior Designer" it was Veronica. She was beautiful.

As I was thinking these things, she looked at my hands and smiled.

"You are an old soul," she said as she studied my hands.

"Why do you say that?" I looked puzzled.

"Your hands look like an old woman owns them," she stated with certainty as she casually took a bite of food.

I took my hands off the table and put them in my lap. I wanted to hide them as fast as I could.

"No, no, don't hide them! It wasn't meant to hurt your feelings. I was trying to say that your hands show you are an old soul who has innate wisdom and knowledge. You should be proud of your hands!" she explained, still with a twinkle in her perfect eyes.

I was 21 with wispy blond hair pulled into pigtails, homemade clothes, a Tennessee accent, and old hands covered in freckles, vein tracks, and dishwater worn. I was the opposite of all that she was and about the last person you would expect to be in a design school filled with designer looking people.

Confidence wasn't my strong suit back then. I never thought of myself as attractive or elegant, and now I had old hands! Who cares if you have wisdom or knowledge when your hands are all anyone is going to see!

Years passed. One evening in my late forties I was on my first date with a very refined man whom I admired. My hair was no longer in pigtails, my jeans came from a department store, and I was in the middle of a career in design.

We were having a nice dinner when I noticed he was looking at my hands. My first thought, "I knew I should have worn those old white gloves of my mother's!"

A smile came across his face.

"I love your hands!" he exclaimed.

Once again, they immediately hid in my lap as I surprisingly replied, "Why?"

"I see character, hard work, and history in those tiny hands," he gently said as he reached out to take one into his.

I didn't date that man long, but I will never forget that moment. I never tried to hide my hands again.

I inherited these old hands from an exceptional group of folks who have the same little tiny, freckled friends I have. My Uncle Paul and I used to laugh that ours were so similar. He was a skilled surgeon whose small hands enabled him to perform intricate surgery long before lasers and robotic instruments were developed for use in the operating room.

Uncle Paul, Dad, and I inherited these hands from my Granny Rose and R. E. Walker. I remember that I always hoped my hands would not look like my Granny's, but they do.

Rose raised her four children with those hands of hers by herself. Her husband, R.E., had died before the smallest was five. And, she was the only one of the bunch who could play the piano and organ efficiently which, in itself, was an anomaly.

Nowadays, my hands match my age. They are even more worn, more freckled and sometimes I still want to find those white gloves.

I was holding my baby granddaughter the other day, and I thought about how many babies these hands have held. How many times have I washed a bottom or a dish or waved goodbye? How many faces have I touched with love and adoration? How many times have I clasped these old hands together in prayer?

My hands have cooked thousands of meals and hammered thousands of nails. These hands cradled my mom the day she died and cradled my children the first day they started to live.

I think we find real beauty in all people in many ways. Yes, you have the glamorous models on shiny magazine covers to show you what beauty is supposed to look like. However, I think real beauty is something far more valuable than what is shown in a magazine.

Perhaps beauty is in the permanent wrinkles around the mouths of people who have laughed through life and brought joy to others. Maybe it is in the stooped woman who once carried the burden of raising her family alone. Perhaps it is in the arthritic football player who once thrilled crowds.

Perhaps it is in the miles we have walked, the tears we have shed, the joy we have shared, the burdens we have carried, and the victories that we enjoyed.

Maybe beauty is in these old hands not for what they look like but for what they have done for this old soul. Perhaps it is time for me to give Mama's old white gloves away.

I Haven't Heard My Name Yet...

I was born into a family that believed one should never sit down, never be lazy, never give up until they called your name from way up yonder!

After 43 years in the physically demanding job of interior designer, I decided to retire. I was the type of designer who did it all myself. Climbed the ladders, hung the pictures, cleaned the shelves, and moved the furniture. Yes, it was physical.

My clients thought I would never sit down. They all figured I would just fall off the ladder one day and be gone. In the back of my mind, I believed they were probably right.

My friend, Ricki, once said, "You will know when it is time to put the hammer down."

"How?" I retorted.

She grinned, "You will just know."

Last September I put the hammer down. I knew. I had moved the last Baby Grand. I had pushed the last sofa. I had climbed the last ladder and dusted the last shelf. It was over.

In my mind, I buried my career in the cemetery and marked it with a beautiful headstone carrying this inscription: "Here's to a career I have dedicated so much of my life to. I am grateful for the pleasure of its work." I left a flower and walked away.

The first reaction to my new-found freedom was to run, not walk, to all the doors that were now open. And, I was so darn grateful that I was still able to do so.

A new level of spiritual energy seeped into my soul. I realized that the senior years were meant not to give up but to give back.

Zest for life is the key to living well. A thirst to stay young, not in looks or athleticism, but in the spirit of our souls.

My friend Deborah and I go to the gym four to five days a week. We've always exercised. Is my body still like a teen's? Heck no!! We workout to be the best we can be at the age we now are. It's just that simple.

We keep moving so that we can continue giving back.

Deborah, a retired social worker, volunteers at the nursing home and never misses a beat when it comes to helping those in need.

My friend Michele is a retired IBM executive who is now a certified, court-appointed advocate to help children of abuse and neglect. All volunteer work.

Ricki, a retired guidance counselor with twelve grandchildren, works with her church. She keeps fit by doing jumping jacks to keep up with all she needs to do.

Tom, a retired engineer, is continuously working on repairs in our neighborhood. A handicapped woman who lives up the street knits blankets for babies and shawls for the elderly. She gives them all away. Her hands keep moving, and her spirit keeps soaring.

To avoid being a grumpy old person, stay a gleeful young person. Who told any of us it was ok to retire from life? Who told any of us to stop giving?

I have a high school friend who retired about the same time as I did. He told me he might wear pajamas all day long. In my mind, I have a picture of him walking around the house and on his beloved golf course in PJs.

Many Sunday mornings I find myself in my pajamas writing an article. Every time I do this, I think about what he said, and I laugh. How youthful and crazy we still are! All my high school buddies are the same. God love them.

John is my age and is about as happy as a clam. He is not retired but is full of smiles and thankful for the grandbabies coming to fill his family with joy.

Yes, some of us aren't yet retired and may never do so. If

you are still working, then show co-workers your wisdom is of value, because it is.

Another high school friend has just completed grueling months fighting cancer. The LaGrange High School class of 1965 has collectively held its breath and given its prayers up for this beloved person. He is on his way back to life! His quote, "If I ever frown again, I told my wife to slap me!" Perfect.

Life is precious. We do need slapping when we think of ourselves as old and finished. When capable of moving, move with enthusiasm. If something aches afterward, take an aspirin. Don't give up.

We need to give back all that we have learned. Give away all the gifts that God has given us. Our talents, our joy, our faith, our love. For our lives are not measured by what we obtain, but by what we give away.

If we can help this world with the time we have left, then don't waste time.

We need to be brave, be bold, be young in spirit, and be of value till they call our name from way up yonder.

I haven't heard my name yet. Have you heard yours?

The Cure For Grumpy Old Folks

The phone rang early one morning over 23 years ago, waking me from a sound sleep.

"Lynn, it's your mother." I have no idea why Mom had to announce who she was, but when she did, I knew it was important.

I sprang off the bed, readying myself for some bad news.

"Well, your Dad is in the car heading to Atlanta!" she stated rather emphatically as if she were a bit miffed.

My parents lived in Crystal River, Florida which is about an eight hour drive from Atlanta. Why was my 81-year-old father driving alone to see me?

Just as I was about to ask my mother that question, she interrupted me and continued with her story.

"Your Dad, (he was mine now, she wasn't claiming him) abruptly decided he wanted to go to Copper Hill, Tennessee to see if he could find some of his old friends."

"Mom, didn't Dad live there when he was about thirteen or fourteen?" I said, now fully awake.

Mom replied, "I told him that idea was crazy and that he should not go, but you know how he is! He left at 5 am."

I did know how he was because I am just like him. Once us Walkers get an idea, there we go. You can't stop us. We are like a freight train on rocket fuel.

I went on to work, and when I arrived home, Dad was sitting at the kitchen table.

"What the heck are you doing, Daddy?" I laughed.

"I am going to spend the night here and head to Copper Hill and find my old friends tomorrow. I want to see if some are still there."

The next morning, he was on the road by six to drive the two hours north.

I arrived home from work late that same afternoon, and there was daddy, again at the kitchen table.

Shocked I said, "Dad, what are you doing back here? Did you not find your friends? Are you ok?!"

"Yep, I found a few," he spoke as he stared at the table looking a bit dejected.

"Well, why didn't you stay for a day or two?" I questioned.

"Oh, heck Lynn, those people are OLD!!!!!!

I laughed so hard I thought I was going to collapse.

Of course, he was the same chronological age as they were, but mentally Dad was still 13. He never saw himself old or grumpy. Yes, he had physical ailments, but they never deterred him from being who he always was.

His spirit roared and laughed all the way to heaven's door.

People have always said, "laughter is the best medicine." I believe that to be true. My family consisted of folks who thought God gave us laughter to help us through the tears and keep us kicking. They exemplified their belief.

How many times have you run across or known grumpy old folks? They worry about everything. They worry about getting to the doctor on time, or are scared to death of dying. How many times have you seen relatively healthy older people sit down, and refuse to get up?

My grandmother always complained about those grumpy types. She would say, "Shoot, don't they know they are gonna die? Why worry about it! They ought to enjoy the livin' till they can't no more!"

She continued, "Why, down at the senior citizen's club, they gave up bowling because they thought they were too old! Shoot, I'm so mad at 'um I could spit! Shoot, I am the oldest one, and I want to bowl!" She was just a hoot and stayed young her entire 97 years.

I have the vaguest memory of my great, great grandmother, Lou Ray Walker, who lived to be almost 100, laughing when she realized I was in the room as Dad held me in his arms. She was blind but knew I was there. Her spirit still could see.

I recall the laughter at family reunions and listening to funny stories about the past. We laughed until our bellies shook and our cheeks turned red just like Santa Claus.

Now that I am in official senior citizen territory along with a bunch of other Baby Boomers, we must keep on laughing. We have to think of ourselves as young, vital, and relevant, as we cackle out loud.

I have told my children if I become grumpy, just slap me silly. I don't want to leave this earth with a frown. I want to depart this life with a laugh just like my Lou Ray who found joy in things she could not even see.

None of us should be so afraid of dying, that we lose the art of living well. We must never think of ourselves as "done."

My cousin Bobby is older than I am by a few years. He is an accomplished attorney still practicing law. He'll send me an email occasionally with a sentence or two that makes me laugh out loud at his humor.

He, along with so many of us, has survived some tough times and tragedies. Sometimes, we have to dig deep to find joy and hope again. Nevertheless, we have to dig. It is our job never to give up, never give in, and never become grumpy and old.

If we do, well, shoot, that would be ridiculous!

The Old Gray Mare And Me

My desk looks like a cyclone ran through it! I am attempting to type amongst a mound of crayons, coloring books, markers, and scattered pieces of torn paper.

My 19-month-old granddaughter is napping now. She will be back at this desk this afternoon to finish her "office work" and art before returning home.

Today is a school holiday. Many grandparents are watching their precious ones while parents work. Next door, my friend, Deborah, is keeping her two grands. Carter and I visited them this morning and enjoyed make believe cookies plus a can of pretend tuna in a play kitchen. Carter tried to cook while holding onto her crayons. She takes her art very seriously.

Over the weekend, my husband and I also watched our other 18-month-old grandson, Mr. Jax. Carter is everything dainty, girly, and artsy, whereas Jax is everything opposite. Just think linebacker on the UGA football team. His bow legs carry his stocky frame that has no clue what fear is. Look for him next year as the newest recruit. He will be the shortest one on the field.

Picking up Jax and Carter is akin to lifting a bowling ball and a feather. And, boy, do they like for me to pick them up! Carter loves me to carry her while getting kisses. Jax wants me to lift him to see what is on the counter, the shelf, or if there is something he needs to fix.

I raised three children, worked full time, cleaned my own home, cooked every meal, and was most recognizable as the mom who had three children attached to her body. I worked out, slept an average of six hours nightly, sewed, wiped away tears, fended off illnesses without extreme fatigue racking my body.

Where the heck is that woman?

Deborah and I still work out and declare we have not changed much since our kids were small. We ignore the mirror on most days and get lost in our world of make believe just like those toddlers in their make-believe kitchen.

Today my body is asking me a serious question: "Are you trying to kill me?" My back is in spasms; moreover my neck is no longer able to carry a brain. My feet ache, and my eyes are half open.

A song keeps floating around in the brain now on the floor: "The Old Gray Mare, she ain't what she used to be many long years ago!"

Nope, I guess she ain't. As much as I hate to admit it, I can no longer do what I used to as a Mom. Age has a way of speaking her mind even though most of the time, I ignore her.

There is a lot I would change about the woman and mother I knew long ago. I would now be more aware of every moment of the three lives hanging onto me. I would listen more intently, have more patience, and hug them even harder. I would be more appreciative of the seconds spent with my family and not worry so much about the seconds missed at my desk.

The bottom line is, I guess that is why there are grandparents. Old Gray Mares may not be what they used to be, but maybe what they lack physically, they make up for in wisdom.

A child knows when you love them enough to let them mess up your desk, floor, or kitchen. They know they are loved when you demand good behavior with soft words. They understand that your time is theirs and nothing can interfere with the pleasure of play.

My oldest granddaughter and I still enjoy a sense of play. She applies my make up and tells me how to work my phone. She is entering the stage of "Oh, Lord, please don't!" Better known as the teenage years. No matter what stage she is in, she knows for sure, this grandma will be there.

There are challenging years ahead for all these precious children. They will rise and fall on many occasions. However, what will temper the fall is the Old Gray Mare's words of encouragement, pure love, and open arms. Those of us that have once carried the weight of the world, still try, even though our backs are swayed, and our brains occasionally fall on the floor.

Do You Hear The Timer Ticking?

There comes a time when you realize with certainty that there is a timer on life. I can't tell you exactly when you'll start to hear it ticking, but be grateful when you do.

We all come face to face with our mortality. My brother died at a relatively young age from a terminal illness. Like many, he was forced to face his limited time. John knew what he wanted to do in the months remaining of his life. As an engineer with a list for everything, he worked hard to complete his tasks and leave this earth to see what was happening on around the bend.

The longer we live, we slowly come to accept that we all have a list to complete, people we need to see, and things we need to say.

Dan had a heart attack last week. Richie is recovering from cancer. Whit had a devastating fall a few years back but, thankfully, survived. Patsy passed away before our last reunion. All of these great folks graduated with me from high school.

I could keep telling you about friends who barely made it or those who did not, but the pages are just not long enough. The older we become, the more we notice the timer as it clicks closer to zero.

Now, that all sounds dour and full of doom, right? Well, maybe, it is all in how we look at it.

I like the timer. I am glad I see it, hear it, and realize that I need to live fully in the seconds that pass.

When I was in high school with Dan, Rich, Whit, and Patsy, I never saw the life clock. Time was infinite in my mind. When several friends sadly died early in life, I would pause and ponder about my mortality. Then life would return to the busy mode, and the sound of the ticking clock would fade away.

For many of us, as time passes, the more we long to see the precious people who have taken up time in our lives. There is an intense desire to share with those we love the depth of that love and how important it is to us.

The seasons of our lives bring changes. I wish I could spend more time with my children now that I have a bit more freedom to do so. However, they are in the busy season of life, and their timers are hidden somewhere under the clutter in their kitchens. They cannot hear the ticking because of the hustle and bustle of their daily lives. I understand because I was once in that season.

I also now understand my mother when she would repeatedly ask, "Are you coming over today?" It was her longing to spend more time with her daughter because there was no longer clutter in her kitchen and she could hear the clocks sweeping hands.

My brother yearned to find his buddies from school, lost cousins, shipmates from his destroyer in Viet Nam, and to spend his last days seeing the faces of his family.

When my son lay on a gurney with a broken neck, he held my hand and urgently told me his wishes as he quickly orated a will. He saw the clock as the second hand moved at a rapid pace. Thankfully, God intervened and gave Corey more time.

Life itself is a rapid movement. We often take it and the folks that are a part of our lives for granted. As we age, we face the quantity of time we have left; we realize how valuable each second, each day, each person, each breath is.

I recall, as if yesterday, watching Dan laugh heartily at a joke in the hall at school. I know it was last week when Richie got me tickled in Latin class. Wasn't it just the other day that Whit was snickering about something crazy I did.... again?! Did I not just see Patsy carrying her books and smiling at me as she strolled into class?

Isn't it today that I find those folks and my memories of them even more precious?

Yes, I am happy to hear the timer. I understand the noises that are important in life. I listen with joy to the laughter of a child. I reach with gladness for the freckled hand of an old friend. I hear God's whispers more often. I see fortune as a miracle and a coincidence as a gift.

Yes, I need to check the time, complete my list, hug those I love with passion, and do so before I continue my journey on around the bend.

Oh, What A Ride!

As a single, working mother with three children, I would often say, "If I can just get my kids through college, everything after that would be like riding a gravy train!"

Little did I know that I would still have to make the gravy, load it on the train, and then engineer the dang thing!

Surprisingly, that old train has taken me to the time of my life.

I must have thought long ago that when my kids left home, I would sit in front of a mirror watching my skin wrinkle as tears rolled down my cheeks. The loss of children living at home and the loss of any looks I ever had were about as far as my thoughts went when I pondered my later years.

Boy was my brain full of gravy!

The senior years are so much more than looks or suffering losses. They are the years that define courage, wisdom, immense love, charity, and finally, boldness.

It is our time to make an old dream come true. It is our time to not only reflect but add new reflections. It is not our time to fade away; it is our time to shine.

It takes work, stamina, and strength to load a train. That is why I lift weights. That is why I try to eat fewer brownies and more berries. Trust me, that is work!

I know folks my age who counted the candles on their birthday cake and then just sat down. The heat must have gotten to them!

My father, Ray, had a massive heart attack when he was sixty-six. As he was recovering in the cardiac care unit, his cardiologist was concerned that after two weeks, they still could not regulate his heart rate.

"I have assured Ray that he is going to live if he lives by the rules. I have told him his life is not over. However, he seems to want to give up," the frustrated doctor explained to my mother and me.

Finally, my Dad asked the doctor the one question that put his heart rate back to normal, "Doc, am I going to be able to play golf again?" You could hear the laughter all over the CCU. After Dad heard "Yes!" he was released from the hospital within two days.

Dad not only played golf again, but he also obeyed the doctor's rules, never sat down, had a few health scares, and laughed his way through life for twenty more years.

I learned from my father to keep moving even when it hurts because it will hurt worse if you sit down.

"Give from your heart until your heart stops," Ray would say.

Dad's humor, his ageless spirit, and his kindness kept him young until his heart, indeed, quit beating.

I have experienced some mighty big punches in life, as most of us have: The loss of my parents and only sibling, a child who fought cancer, another in a horrible accident, friends who left long before I was ready to say goodbye, and that was all after becoming a card-carrying senior.

At times the train seemed to derail, but what put it back on track was a tremendous amount of faith and an immeasurable amount of love. Bad things can stop a train; the trick is to keep loading it with enough hope and courage to fire up the engine again eventually.

The senior years are not easy, but after you have witnessed living for a while, the wisdom you gain is deep and profound. It IS to be passed along, shared and respected.

When I became the engineer of my train, I realized I could choose the track I wanted to be on. There is no right or wrong way to go unless I decide to stop before reaching my destination.

When I am not sure which route to take, I ask my boss who lives where my parents and brother reside. I learned early in life that if God gives you a voice, a task, or a thought, do what He says. Make a difference.

There was a voice in my heart the minute I retired, a nagging, nudging, nuisance. One day, I went to my computer and wrote a sentence that became a published story, which became a weekly column, which became a new career.

That old train took me to the absolute realization that my life is by no means over because I have a lot to do before it is. I need to give back and leave a legacy that inspires the ones just boarding the train.

I have survived fearful things, so now I am not afraid.

I am not afraid to try and fail. I am not scared to say and write what I feel. I am not afraid to reach out or reach up.

What do I have to lose? Time is a gift, so why waste it?

We all must keep the train gliding along its track to experience one fantastic, often arduous, journey.

Yesterday taught me how to be who and what I am today: bold, complete and immensely thankful.

I wouldn't trade that for all the youth elixirs in China.

Lessons

Life has a way of teaching us a new lesson every day. As we age, we tend to believe we know it all; there is nothing more to learn.

However, if we view our days as opportunities to be taught new lessons, gain wisdom as well as insight, we continue to grow no matter our age.

We are never too old to improve the quality of our lives and become the best version of ourselves.

So stay in school, keep listening to the Teacher until the final bell rings, calling you home.

The Lesson From The Old Man In A Faded Suit

He was walking toward me on a side street in Charleston, SC. I could see him from far away as his faded, old mocha brown suit hung loosely from his stooped shoulders. His presence, such a contradiction to the bright sun beaming down on the colorful window boxes that adorn Queen Street where the sweet scent of their flowers filled the morning air. The man's black tie and white shirt were in contrast to his dark brown skin and graying black hair. He tipped his head as he approached, and then stopped to smile at the four friends who were visiting his town on this bright April day.

"Ma'am, do you think you could spare some change for a sandwich?" he asked as he flashed a semi-toothless smile.

I reached for my wallet and realized I only had a dollar bill, a twenty, and some change.

I rustled through all the change and gave it to him along with the dollar.

The others in the group did as well.

"Thank you, ma'am." The old man bowed his head and then ambled away.

The girls and I went on to an excellent restaurant for brunch. It was our last day in Charleston. We had enjoyed three days of eating, sipping wine, laughing, walking, and touring in perfect weather. It had been a great girl's trip.

As I sat in the restaurant that morning, my mind returned to the man in the faded suit. "Why did I not give him the twenty? I didn't have to order this brunch. Lord knows I don't need it! I should have given him the twenty and ordered toast and coffee!" I said to myself as I bantered aloud with my friends about how beautiful our trip had been.

Charleston, with its church spires that rise to the heavens and are surrounded by the graves of Southern royalty, is known as the Holy City of America. Rainbow Row and the Battery evoke awe as one gazes upon the architectural splendor of beautiful homes.

Streets of cobblestone, exquisite food, and equally lovely gardens create charm amid restored row houses and mansions. The ocean glimmers in the sun as you spot Ft. Sumter in the distance.

Ft. Sumter, where the Civil War began. This same ocean carried slaves onto the cobblestone streets to be sold to work on the plantations, tend the exquisite gardens and cook the plentiful food in the kitchens of those grand houses.

After the Civil War started on that fateful day in Charleston, after over 618,000 soldiers gave their lives, and after the slave markets closed, Charleston experienced decay.

Earthquakes and neglect shook the spires of the churches, and many of the mansions gave way to rubble and ruin. It would take almost 150 years before Charleston was again known as one of the best cities in America.

Racism, injustice, intolerance, insensitivity, and neglect will destroy a city, and us. God teaches us that giving to the poor and being compassionate is far more honorable than living in a big house. He has shown us time and time again throughout history that lack of compassion for others and decadence cause where we live and who we are to reduce to dust.

Have we become so jaded by swindlers and criminals that we can no longer detect a person in need? Have we become judge and jury of every life that passes by us because they are in faded suits or are different than us?

I realized as I sat in the restaurant that healing begins with me. I must become more aware, with eyes wide open, to see and discern need in another human being. I have been poor without a faded suit. I have been alone on a crowded street without being homeless. I, too, have begged to be noticed and longed to be loved without asking.

Yes, I worked my way through it, but what if the opportunity had never knocked on my door? Would I have become one asking for change on the street?

Many go by a rule to never give to someone on the street. I understand the argument. However, I can only say that when you feel a need in your heart to help even one person, it is from a higher power than a "rule."

God says that the poor will always be among us and so will those who turn their eyes away from them. Perhaps the sinner is not the one in the mocha brown suit; perhaps the sinner is the one who started to pass the old man. The sinner is the one who gave only the change and not the twenty. The sinner is me.

I am going back to Charleston one day. I will walk down Queen Street, and when I find my friend in the wrinkled shirt, old suit, with his toothless smile, I am going to thank him for teaching me a valuable lesson.

While richness and beauty surrounded me in the Holy City, holiness is giving to the outstretched hand of another. Human kindness is the one thing that will keep Ft. Sumter quiet, the church spires looming to the sky, and keep all of us humble.

Meanwhile, I owe a man a $20 bill.

Do Our Eyes Cause Impaired Vision?

When my granddaughter was three, I asked her how old her Mother was.

"Ten!" she replied with certainty.

"Your Father?"

"Ten, too!" was her absolute answer.

"Well, then Avery, how old am I?"

Without looking up to my face, she answered, "You are three, just like me!"

Avery saw me through the bright eyes of a child. She had deduced that I was her age because I would play with her, converse with her on her level, and was her best friend. I was three, just like her.

Children teach us valuable lessons in life. They judge not by what they are told or physically see, but rather by what they feel in their innocent hearts.

As we age, we begin to see things we didn't notice before. People look differently in our eyes. We are often guilty of grouping folks into categories and often find it difficult to see beyond the category. People are conservative **or** liberal, wealthy **or** poor, black **or** white **or** Hispanic and never anything outside the handy label we assign to them.

Have you ever noticed that once you get to know someone well, you are no longer aware of the difference that you initially saw with your eyes? I recall going back to college in the 70s when I was a young mother. We lived in Birmingham, Alabama and since I had left high school, times had changed. I was now in an integrated school population for the first time. I always thought racial divide was stupid in the first place, so I was very comfortable with my new world.

There was a young lady who had every class with me since we had the same major. We became fast friends. She and I were walking across the quadrangle on a hot spring day rushing to our next class. She was drinking a bottled cola as we walked.

"May I have a sip?" I asked as I grabbed it out of her hand. Since she had not offered to share, I laughingly said as I took the sip, "How rude are you anyway?!"

She stopped dead still as I strolled on blabbing with her coke in my hand. It took me a minute before I realized she wasn't at my side. "Gloria, come on we are going to be late!" She was still not moving, just staring at me. "I'm sorry I took your drink; I was just kidding!"

"No, Lynn, that's not it. You drank after me!" she said with tears brimming in her eyes.

"I don't understand, are you sick?" I questioned.

"No, I am black!"

With all the emotion that was happening between us at the moment, God gave me the perfect response, "Gee, I hadn't noticed." She cried all the way to class as I put my arm around her.

I had forgotten that she was different from myself. Her color was the only difference, though. What lay beneath her skin was a beautiful girl who was just my friend.

How many times have we been afraid of a person, because they just didn't "look right?" How many times have we passed by someone that could have used our help? How many times have our eyes failed us? How many opportunities for friendship and understanding have we missed because we judged with our eyes?

My granddaughter is now twelve. She is still my best friend, but now knows how much older I really am. She teases me about it a lot. When I visit her, I always lie down with her in the dark of the night. She cannot see, and that is when she and I talk. She tells me everything about her world. You know, in the dark, she can now see that I am just…twelve.

The Call To Goodness

Have you ever noticed that when there is a catastrophe, either caused by nature or by humans, a strange thing occurs?

After 9/11, people of all ages, all colors, all religions, and all political beliefs gathered to raise the flag, went to war, and united to fight a mortal enemy. We prayed, we suffered, and we held onto each other.

After Hurricane Katrina, people of all ages, all colors, all religions, and all political beliefs gathered to find folks shelter, gave money, and united to rebuild a part of our nation that was devastated by nature.

In Texas, people of all ages, all colors, all religions, and all political beliefs endured danger to pull others from flood waters caused by Hurricane Harvey. They prayed for those missing and lifted each other up after suffering enormous loss.

In the middle of crisis or war, no one sees color, age, or beliefs.

When it gets right to the core of survival, we must be rising to the call of our inherent goodness. Right?

Why would God still be hanging on to us? Perhaps, He still sees that we are worthy of His grace and His forgiving love. He understands, as we all should, that we need each other. When we save another, fight for another, or feed another, we become children of God. It is who we are and what we need to remember in all that we do.

I am a huge sinner. I am keenly aware of my pitfalls, and I know I have made God cry on more than a few occasions. However, I also know that somewhere within me is the person who would go barefoot in the flood waters to save a child, a friend, a stranger, or even a pet.

We had a little get together with friends over the Labor Day weekend in our neighborhood. Judy was not able to attend.

She was in a hospital bed with a heart issue as well as pneumonia. Our thoughts were with Judy and her husband as we gathered on a beautiful, starry night.

"Let's say a prayer for Judy," the host implored. The party silenced as heads bowed.

"We need to organize and prepare dinners for a while after they return home," Barbara stated as she searched for pencil and paper.

All volunteered. All became one to help another in need.

Some folks believe we are all rotten to the core. They find our fundamental good has been engulfed by materialism, by selfishness, and by greed. Frankly, sometimes when I watch the news, I come to think that myself.

When tragedy or calamities occur, either in our own lives or our collective lives, we rise to the standard to which God calls us to be. The golden rule becomes viable and visible, shining like a beacon.

We see goodness every day. It does not make the local news at five, but at six there are people still bringing dinners to friends who have fallen ill. Friends and strangers are rushing to the aid of those who have found trouble or are in crisis. All day, people are asking God for mercy, healing, and help.

The good in us should strive to stand tall against evil, fight injustice, and continue to pull others out of the floods of sadness that engulf so many. We should always be ready to answer the call.

There is a hero in each of us. There is power in our hearts. There is a light within our darkness and hope that genuinely does spring eternal. When we see soldiers battle in a war, or neighbors pull folks out of harm's way, or those with opposing political views and beliefs write a check to aid the downtrodden, we witness good.

The floods will recede. The towns will rebuild. The wars will be won or lost. We will forget the pictures of folk's heroism and goodwill. We will once again battle over our varying points of view.

Our politicians will continue to belittle themselves and us on occasion. We will disappoint others, ourselves, and God often. Our altruism will be set on the backburner while our selfishness will be stewing in a pot and our inherent goodness will be in the warming drawer.

However, there will be another crisis. There will be another friend in need, and there will also be a voice within that becomes loud and mighty.

It is the call to goodness, and, rest assured, we as a people of all ages, all colors, all religions, and all political beliefs...will answer.

Where To Find Light On Dreary Days

Some days seem plain gloomy. Days when you wake up feeling out of sorts or out of fuel. Today is one of those days, but I haven't a clue as to why. Could it be the unfair five pounds I put on every year right before swimsuit season? Could it be my oldest child will turn the age I believe I am next week or could it be the rain? I feel homesick, but I am home! I think I am suffering from "yuckiness!"

The cartoon "Garfield" did make me laugh this morning when his owner, Jon, read him a bedtime story which was the recipe for lasagna! Actually, reading my recipe sounded like a good idea until I concluded I would probably put on another pound just reading the ingredients. I saw another cartoon about a dog celebrating his birthday, and then I remembered I really couldn't be the same age as my child, could I?

Ok, the cartoons weren't helping the dreariness!

Then I thought, "I'll give myself a facial. I will lift my gloomy face to youthfulness with one of those dollar cucumber masks!" I washed my face, looked in the mirror and decided the world does not produce enough cucumbers to lift the fallen whatever it is the mirror is reflecting.

Ok, the mask was a bad idea unless I put a cloth mask over my eyes and go back to bed.

Oops, I need to wash the sheets. The smell of fresh linens usually makes me feel better. I always hated to wash clothes when the kids were little, but now it is my favorite chore to do. Why did those kids grow up? I need them to come back now that I enjoy doing laundry.

Ok, now I know why I feel homesick. I want to go back to the house where all the kids ran around my yells, where the washing machine spun all day, where I apparently left my face, and I was the same age as my daughter is now.

I don't think I will wash those sheets.

My friend Ricki came over for dinner the other night and brought me a new devotional book, Jesus Always by Sarah Young, as a gift. Perhaps I need to find wisdom through words other than Garfield's.

The first sentence I read in the little book said, "I am God, your joy, and your delight. Knowing I am your joy can protect you from bemoaning your circumstances or envying others whose situations seem better than yours."

I turned around immediately to see if the Lord was standing in the kitchen cooking lasagna! How did He know I needed to hear those words? Oh, yeah, my gloomy yuckiness was not allowing me to see His joy which only required a bit of stirring.

After reading and praying a bit, I realized the only way I am going to fit in that bathing suit is to quit eating so much! You know the only way to lift my face off the floor is to smile? And, you know the only way to not miss my children is to embrace the years they have called me "mom" and to know one of them is now my age!

I believe God throws us dreary days occasionally to teach us to search for sunshine within. It is there where we find God's light. He reminds us He is always standing in the kitchen or anywhere we are. He knows the sadness in our hearts or the unexplainable gloom in our souls. When we don't understand it, He does. That alone is worth being joyful.

The house is quiet, and as I write, I realize writing was not on my agenda today. Here in my office is where God sends me to find joy. I didn't connect those dots until now. He knew through His words of wisdom, His comfort, and His support; I would find sunshine in the place I always do, right here where my soul pours words on paper.

Ok, I am all better now. Maybe I'll try that facial again, do some sit-ups, wash those sheets, and thank God for bringing sunshine into my kitchen today.

Political Correctness vs. Human Kindness

Have you ever thought that if we practiced being kind, we wouldn't need "Political Correctness?" The term "Political Correctness" seems shallow to me. We are to stop and think about the group we could be offending before we speak. Kindness, however, should be with us in a more soulful place to cause us not to hurt anyone.

My Grandmother was just the best person I have ever known. She was what we call, "the salt of the earth." Humble beginnings, humble spirit, and humble to all people and God. She quietly made her mark on this world through the generations that followed.

When I was a little girl, she taught me a life lesson that has stayed with me. Long ago in the small towns of Tennessee, men would gather around the courthouse on Saturdays while the women shopped. They would whittle wood, smoke pipes, and usually, the talk was about the Bible and politics.

Since everyone knew I never had a shy bone in my body, I would join the men and start conversing as if I were one of them. Once I came across a man who was dirty, and he reeked of alcohol. I went to my Grandmother quickly and told her about the man. I just didn't understand how he could be so "icky."

"Well, Lynn, you see before you can rule him a bad man, you have to walk a mile in his shoes. You never know where he has traveled in those shoes and what he experienced while he was there." As she said that, she reached into her purse and pulled out her change, handed it to me and instructed, "Go over and give him this and say, 'God Bless'."

That is Human Kindness. If we start teaching kindness, along with humility and gentleness, to young children, these traits will likely become an integral part of who they are. I think every one of us desires to be kind but competition, the need for control, needing to be "right," and the feeling that someone "owes" us something are drowning the spirit of kindness.

Kindness has everything to do with how you interact with folks. It is the core of your altruism, it is a grounding rod for faith, and it is the mark you will leave on this earth.

I am appalled at the politicians who make a claim they believe in God, yet slam a competitor with vitriol. Listening to the news media talk shows mortifies me when I hear the hatred thrown, not to a group, (because that would be politically incorrect) but to a person with force. That is unkindness.

I feel condescended to when I am expected to vote for leaders because they try to convince me, through rhetoric, that another candidate is horrible. I am not an idiot, and I doubt you are either. We are not barbaric; we are civilized. We have gone to school, and most of us have been "raised better than that." I turn off the radio when I hear vitriol. I don't vote for people who think I have no understanding of humanity. We all would prefer to understand how a candidate would lead the country rather than how they can destroy the citizens of it.

If political correctness is a new dominant term, and kindness is trivial and "namby-pamby," then let's ask God to define the terms. What do you think He would say?

Many years back I worked for a little bank with nine employees. The president of the bank was also the head of the Democratic Party of Georgia. (Let me interject here, I am an Independent and always have been.)

Politicians visited him on a regular basis. Mr. Farr was like a second father to me at that time, and he needed to be because I never could balance my cash box! He chose me to greet people as they walked through the door because he knew I loved folks, not math.

One day a gentleman came to my teller window and said, "I have a lunch meeting with Mr. Farr." He gave me his name, and I summoned my boss. I thought they were going to the little diner down the street as usual. Once the pair had retreated to an office, I went to the tiny closet breakroom in the back.

The room consisted of a two-seater chrome and vinyl sofa, a card table with a coffee pot and a student fridge underneath it. I pulled out my loaf of white bread, banana, mayo and a small bag of chips and started to prepare my lunch.

Just as I was peeling the banana, Mr. Farr poked his head through the door and questioned, "Do you have enough lunch that we might share?"

"I thought you were going to the diner and eat fried chicken! I only have one banana, mayo, some slices of white bread, and a few chips."

"Ok, that is good, we have enough to make that work!" he said. At that point I thought, well, there went my lunch and started to walk back to my teller window.

"No, Lynn, don't go, we are going to share!"

"Yes," the other gentleman stated, "just slice the banana thin, and we can do it."

I prepared three sandwiches out of that lone banana, put them on our paper plates and started to take my plate to my station where I planned to eat my lunch discreetly.

"No, no, stay with us. We can make room on the sofa," Mr. Farr said as he stopped me. I wedged myself between the two of them. We discussed the political realm of Georgia and poured over wallet photos of our visitor's children.

I listened intently and realized it was way past my lunch hour, but Mr. Farr would not let me leave. Finally, we walked back to the lobby.

The visitor hugged me goodbye. He was a kind man. He had not minded at all when I gave my input even though I was just a slightly grown kid.

As he walked toward the doors to leave, I turned toward my

teller station, but Mr. Farr grabbed my arm. "Lynn, watch him walk through the door, remember today because one day you will be able to tell your grandchildren about this."

The visitor was Jimmy Carter, and Mr. Farr thought that he might go to the top of the political stairs.

Now, a lot of folks never considered Jimmy Carter to be a great President. However, there are not many who would argue the fact that he is kind. Mr. Farr, a kind man, cared about a 21-year old's future memories more than he cared about me missing half an hour at the teller window.

Political correctness was not a term either of them used. You see, these two kind gentlemen didn't need to.

What I Learned From Alex

Alex Hitchcock was seven and moving to New Jersey for the second time in his young life. I was hired by his parents as their Interior Designer when Alex was nine months old, and they resided in Atlanta. This would be the fourth house I was involved with and the second one in New Jersey.

Basking Ridge, New Jersey is a quaint, peaceful town forty miles from Manhattan, soaked in green, covered with deer, and yummy food from local delis and pizza parlors. Shannon, Alex's mom, is an author and former North Carolinian who loves sweet tea and lard biscuits which makes her an extraordinarily lovely person in my book.

The house they bought was an older home which needed a lot of tender loving care. (In design-speak that means renovation.) Since Alex's parents were having to live in a hotel for most of the summer during the remodeling, it was decided that Alex should stay with his grandparents in North Carolina.

That was fine by Alex. He would be on a farm, have grandma's fried chicken and most anything else he wanted. Why would he not be excited over that decision?

While on the farm his grandfather, "Pa Max," gave Alex money for helping with the daily chores. Alex saved each dollar until he had a stack of bills he could hardly carry.

I spent much of the summer planning the renovation and traveling to New Jersey to help Shannon. We changed Alex's little bedroom into a larger room by taking down a wall to an adjoining room. There was now enough space to add a study, play area, and bookshelves. We chose a western theme for the décor with blue walls, using denim, accents of red, burlap, and a bandana print fabric.

Once he arrived from the farm to begin school in Basking Ridge, the house was livable, but not quite finished. The kitchen was not yet operational causing the family to order in or dine out every night.

Shannon heard Alex on the phone one evening whispering to his grandfather in North Carolina. "Pa Max, can you come and get me?" he asked.

"Why?" His grandfather asked, terribly concerned.

"Because these people don't feed me right!" Alex shouted.

Before Alex called Children Services declaring neglect, I arrived to finish the décor, the kitchen was in working order, and Alex was happy with his new school because they served a good pizza for lunch.

I started putting books on his shelves and curtains on his windows. His toys were neatly organized, and his room was becoming as unique as he was.

I finally finished the house, and I was ready to fly home early one morning. When I walked down the hall towing my luggage, I heard footsteps behind me.

"Miss Lynn, wait!" Alex shouted.

I turned to see Alex with his little pajamas resting on top of his bare feet and his bowl cut bangs were disheveled from a night of sleeping in his cowboy room.

"Here Miss Lynn, I want to give you this," he quietly said as he held up so many dollar bills that it took both of his hands to hold them. I quickly realized it was all the money his Pa Max had given him throughout the summer.

I leaned down to meet him eye to eye. "Alex, why would you want to give me all the dollars you earned and saved?

He sweetly replied, "You worked hard and made my room so pretty. You need to be paid for all of the stuff you did!"

I placed the money back in his hands and explained to him that his parents were paying me, so he didn't need to use his money.

After I convinced him to keep his two hundred dollars, I hugged him tightly and said goodbye. I watched him as he shuffled back to his room to hide his money safely.

Alex is now 25, a graduate of American University and working in Alexandria, Virginia. I think of him often and pray the passage of years hasn't taken away the giving nature of this special little boy as it does so many of us.

Oh, the heart of a child and his humble, giving spirit. Oh, the gift of the child who believes without complication or hesitancy. Oh, the innocence found in a child who is content with piece of fried chicken and a dollar.

The Bible teaches that we must become like a child to enter the kingdom of Heaven. We must put the hoarding of pride, the discontent, the cynicism, and any mean spirit within us, away. As adults, we must dig deep to find our inner child and become more like Alex who was willing to give all he had because he believed it was only right to do so.

Treasures

We all possess things we love. For some, it may be a car, a painting, a comfy chair, or a set of golf clubs. I have found even though I do love many things, it is the old items which tell a story or recount a memory that become priceless treasures.

It is the old stuffed bear from childhood, a grandmother's necklace, or a love letter that will stir our emotions.

The rocking chair where mother cradled us or the antique table we gathered around inspires us to keep telling the stories of a family to the next generation.

These treasures always bring a smile to our face and comfort to our hearts.

These "Things" I love

I got a new car this year. I adore my car, but this is not one of the "things" I genuinely love. Oh, it is shiny, gadget-filled, and is indeed unique, but not as special as the old spinning wheel in the hall.

The spinning wheel crafted by the hands of my great, great grandfather in the 1800s remains as it was then. The worn sides are a reminder of the generations of women who spun the yarn with their feet propped up on its edge. It reminds me that not so long ago there was no JoAnn's or Walmart to run to for yarn and fabric.

When my children were small they used the old wheel for playing the "Price is Right" right in our living room. As they aged, my children swore it moved one night by itself, declaring it haunted. I prefer to think it was James Randolph returning to ensure the wheel was still in working order.

In the dining room are a Blue Willow vegetable bowl, two chipped Blue Willow dishes and a platter proudly displayed among cheap copies of delftware. Under the lid of the old bowl is a note:

"Please care for these pieces. They belonged to our family in the 1800s who immigrated from Great Britain."

Every time I admire those items I think of the sacrifices that many families made to come to America. The fear of facing the unknown with children in tow and faith in abundance. I run my hands across the chips and look at the perfect condition of the bowl and am awed that they survived all the years. How humbled I am to be the caretaker of these priceless items for a while.

The lamp in the foyer is a treasure. It was initially a kerosene lamp that lit the way for past generations. The cut crystal bowl at the top is exquisite and delicate. Every time I clean it, I'm scared to death I'll break it. The lamp came over on the boat with a family pursuing a dream. I can imagine one of my ancestors wrapped a cloth over and around the crystal to protect it. I am sure she worried about its safety. Every time I pass the lamp, I think of her. I make a silent promise to continue to worry about it.

On my old hutch, worn and damaged from the flood my parents endured one year, is my Dad's fishing creel he inherited from one of his relatives. It is now over 150 years old. Beside it is a picture of my father as a very young man holding a largemouth bass he caught at the Monterey Lake in the town where I was born in Tennessee.

How many times did Dad fish in the lake which was owned by his uncles? How many times did he rub the leather straps with conditioning oil to protect them? To this day the old creel is magnificent. It reminds me of the father who never took for granted any "thing" he ever owned.

The hand-carved dough bowl was made by the same person who crafted the spinning wheel. I can still see my great-grandmother in the kitchen with flour up to her little elbows. The wood burning stove is behind her, and she is kneading biscuits using the old bowl which belonged to her mother.

Her bun is at the nape of her neck, and her apron soiled from all the dishes she is preparing to serve after church. How great is that old bowl?

As far back as I can remember my family treasured the treasures of their heritage. They protected and cherished the things they had and then passed them down the family line. From fry pans to crystal, from photos to a washstand or a treasured book. These items reflect the stories of pioneers, hard workers, and courageous people.

Yes, I have some shiny new things, but it is the things from yesterday that are my most valuable treasures. They remind me of those who paved the way for me to have the life I have now and to be very grateful for my ancestors.

My daughter, Amy, has her grandmother's letter sweater from high school mounted and framed. My daughter, Heather, has the dining table my uncles and father made the year I was born. My son, Corey, has his grandfather's hats and pocket knives.

The tradition of valuing the real meaningful material things in life continues.

My great, great grandfather must have a smile on his face every time I polish the old spinning wheel and dust the shelves where pictures of his children and grandchildren reside.

We all love "things." I find it is the sentimental items which touch our hearts that are the most valuable. The cars, clothes, and stylish trinkets will come and go. The pictures, old family Bibles, a grandmother's ewer, a love letter, or an old spinning wheel turn our lives to the past and remind us that the lives who cherished those "things" are priceless.

The Table

As an interior designer, I was invited into many residences over the years. I would advise clients how to turn their houses into homes. I found that whether it was a bungalow or a mansion, the most significant piece of furniture was always the dinner table or "supper table" as we called it when I was young.

I was sitting in my kitchen the other day, and I realized my supper table needed a makeover. My husband and I spent the weekend sanding, painting, creating a new look for our eating area. It turned out beautifully, and we were giving each other "high fives."

David, my husband, returned to his recliner to watch a ball game as I put the final wax on the table top. I looked at the old hutch that resides next to the table. On its top shelf sits my grandmother's tea pitcher next to a vase my mother loved. On the second shelf, lives a crazy ceramic fish my son made in school many years ago. There is also a picture of my father as a young man holding a large bass he just caught. The bottom shelf holds my father's 150-year-old creel trimmed in rich, brown leather. Plates scatter in between pictures and mementos.

I sat down in one of the chairs and stared at my old "new" table and the hutch holding its treasury of yesterday. My mind raced back to when my children were small.

When they were growing up, I implemented one of my smartest "Mom" rules. "No TV or phone calls allowed during meals" unless something extraordinary was on. I would encourage all new parents to adopt this rule. The reward is priceless

My children all have tables of their own now, but there was a time when all of life happened around this table. The table where kids threw books at the end of a school day. The table where homework would eventually get finished. The table where little children wrinkled their noses at anything green and everything required catsup.

As they grew, somene else's children also sat at the table. It seemed as though every night one of my children brought a friend home to eat with us. I remember once when my son was beginning high school, I didn't recognize the face across from me.

"Hello," I said, "and who are you?"

Corey interrupted, "Oh, Mom, this is Ray! He heard you were a great cook, so I asked him over!"

Those kids knew they could win me with a compliment like that. We clasped our hands, blessing our food. We laughed, we ate, we talked about what was up among the group while our dog made the rounds under each foot begging for food. A typical evening in our home. Chaotic, unusual, and usually hilarious.

Coming home from a mission trip a few years later, Ray was killed in the Value Jet crash over the Florida Everglades. I am glad he visited our table. I am thankful all those kids who came over to share a meal felt at home, and called me, "Miss Lynn."

Many hard talks happened around our supper table. Many tears were shed on its top, many heartaches worked out, many chapters turned, much laughter shared. There have been numerous prayers prayed while clasping the hands of those who will never return. But, I am so thankful that I got to hold these hands: The hand of my grandmother who poured the tea, the hand of the father who caught the big bass and the hand of the mother who put flowers in the pretty vase.

In every home I entered during my career, I watched how people gathered around the table. It was all the same. It seems that those who took the time to unite around this workhorse of furniture had the closest of relationships. No TV or phone to distract this precious time to communicate, to love, to forge and seal a memory to be shared in later years.

All of my children came home at Christmas. A few weeks ago there were twenty family members gathered to eat supper. It was so loud, and laughter so boisterous I thought that table was going to move right out the door! Then they were gone. Silence and empty chairs were all that remained.

At first, I was sad until I looked at a piece of art that hangs above the hutch. My mother bought it one day in an antique store for fifty cents. It is a small wood etching of a man sitting at a dinner table with twelve of his followers with whom to share His last supper.

After studying His face, His hands outstretched, His disciples listening intently, I was no longer sad. I knew He had blessed our family with precious times around our supper table.

The Superstorm And The Hutch

There is an old hutch in our breakfast room that needs refinishing. Every time I go to get the sandpaper, I wind up putting it back in my tool bin. This old, worn, cherry hutch tells a story of survival, hardship, and two people whose lives were saved because they once owned it.

It was March 1993; my parents had moved from LaGrange to Crystal River, Florida twenty years earlier. Dad had left Georgia to manage the development of a cluster home community four miles west of Crystal River toward the Gulf of Mexico.

For years the community was idyllic. The waters from the gulf wrapped around seawalls surrounding the community. The land was flat and the ocean calm. Fish jumped, dolphins played, frogs croaked, and crabs scampered.

My children and I spent all our vacations at my parent's fun residence. Both of my Dad's brothers bought homes there and retired. The brothers told stories and laughed at their own youthful memories as the kids played and created their own.

Then the winds came and the sea churned as if Mother Nature flew into a rage.

It was simply called "The Storm of the Century." It was caused by cyclonic activity in the distant waters of the Gulf of Mexico. Before it finished its destructive path, it had caused 12-foot storm surges as it hit the Gulf's sandy beaches. More had drowned from this storm's rage than from Hurricanes Hugo and Andrew combined. As the storm made its way up the eastern seaboard, it created snow and ice storms, spawned tornados, knocked out power to ten million people, and affected the lives of forty percent of all American citizens.

On the morning of March 13, 1993 many people who lived in the community Dad managed, evacuated. They left everything. Some were taken by helicopter and others by military transport.

My parents decided to stay. My 79-year-old father felt responsible for others and, foolishly, thought he could save their property and belongings. A strong man with a heart condition was determined to save the day! Funny how our minds have no concept of what we can withstand.

The water started to rise at an alarming rate. They piled furniture as high as they could. They went door to door to make sure all were either gone or safe.

When the water reached their waist inside their home, the highest place they could find was atop the beautiful cherry hutch mother had bought in the 1950s. They precariously sat on its top ledge and held on to each other.

Finally, some folks found them and moved them to a safe place.

My phone rang. It was the first time I ever heard panic in my mother's voice and shaking in the words my father spoke. I began to cry.

Ice was starting to form on the power lines as I looked out my window in Atlanta. There was no way to reach them, help them, or begin to understand what they had just gone through.

Mother Nature had just created the Storm of the Century and ended the idyllic life my parents had known. Mom no longer wanted to stay in Florida and no amount of comfort could ease her fear. We all understood.

By the time they moved to Atlanta, many of their possessions had been given away. The only furniture they brought were the pieces they loved, yet were damaged from the flood.

Especially the old hutch. Its legs were bleached and dry. A door didn't quite shut all the way. The drawers stuck a bit and salt water had dulled its hardware.

"I figured I would fix her up and use her anyway. She is one piece of furniture I couldn't part with. That old hutch saved our lives!" she would say as she decorated its shelves and put oil on its poor legs.

When my mother died, I inherited the old hutch. I often sit and gaze at the unscratched panes of glass in the top doors and wonder how they did not break. I always am trying to keep that bottom door shut. I keep adding more oil to the old legs that held up my mom and dad as the water rose around them.

Sixty-two years ago, the furniture store delivered the most beautiful piece of furniture I had ever seen. Mama was so proud to own it. Dad was happy for her. She filled it with her china, and kept it polished with her lemon oil.

Today, even with her damaged legs, her door that never shuts, she stands regal, beautiful, and proud. She is a reminder of the survival, courage and strength of the people she saved and the parents I loved.

There are some things even floods can't wash away.

My Writing Place

If I could, I would bring all of you here to this place where I write my stories. It isn't at all what I imagined it would be in my dreams.

I knew long ago that when I could, I would devote my time to writing. I would set up a room with light yellow walls and sheer curtains that would gently billow as the spring air blew through an open window.

The room would be a haven of quiet for me to ponder my thoughts before putting them on paper. Pink and yellow roses would sit at my desk and rich pine floors would be under my feet.

Funny thing about dreams like that, they usually stay dreams.

Instead, a beige carpet adorned with dots of spilled coffee is under my feet. The walls are a deeper beige color that I once loved, but now loathe.

I painted it myself when we first moved into this house, and believe me, you can tell.

It is by far the ugliest, messiest room in our home. My husband works a great deal from here so we share this mixed-up space.

This large room boasts a dormer window with enough space in front of it for my pub table which serves as my desk. My space is always cluttered with files, dictionaries, coffee cups and bills I really need to pay.

In the main area of the room, a bed awaits in one corner to serve as a spillover respite for guests.

My husband's desk is quite ugly, but serves its purpose. And, of course, he bought the ugly file cabinet, bookshelf, and chair to match.

As a retired interior designer, let me assure you, this is a designer's legit nightmare.

I look to the left around my little space as the light filters through the dusty blinds and see a poem that my older daughter wrote when she went on a trip to Maine. She attached photos of Acadia National Park, framed it, and gave it to me as a gift long ago.

Underneath is a picture of my seven-year-old son, resting his head on my shoulder. I swear that picture is a photo of pure love. One of my favorites.

Above the coffee cups on my desk are an array of photos with mismatched frames. There is one of my granddaughter playing in the sand when she was two, several of my three children as babies and teenagers, one of my nephew, Alex, as a college man, and one of my grandmother playing Chinese checkers.

Hanging on a door is my son's old hat he refused to take off as a young boy. Red, white, and dirty, but would I ever clean it? No.

There is a crazy looking four-foot-tall carved wooden giraffe in the corner. Ralph's eyes stare at me daily. "Are you ever going to clean this place up?" His eyes search mine for an answer.

Above the left corner of my pub table is a tiny plaque that reads, "Let us be silent that we may hear the whisper of God." I put it there to remind me to be quiet, because unless you remind me, I won't.

I would take you elsewhere in this room but it only gets worse.

The rest of the house has been culled to my idea of beauty. It soothes my eyes and reminds me of a career that spanned the better part of my life.

However, this messy olio where I sit now soothes my heart. I find God's whispers here along with memories captured in frames, poems and a child's hat. Even my coffee cups are treasures. A beauty that contains a bit of stale tea from yesterday was a gift from my granddaughter at Christmas. The yellow Wonder Woman cup holding cold coffee was given to me by special friends when my daughter was sick and they thought us brave. I treasure it.

When my husband isn't asking me how to spell something, I can lose myself in these words on paper, and find myself when I look at those I love.

God put me in this cubby to remind me that beauty to the eye is not as wonderful as peace in the heart.

I adore the whispers I hear, and the mess that I make. My ugly room is my favorite place in this house. It is where I belong. It is where my heart lies, and my past and future collide.

Everyone has a special place. It could be a closet, a swing on a porch, a chair by a lake, or the ugliest room in the house. It is there that you will hear the whispers in the silence. It is there that you will find true beauty and peace.

Visit it often.

My writing place!

America

God blessed me when He determined I would be born on American soil. My ancestors explored this land after they arrived in 1649 to settle in a country established on dreams.

Many of them fought and died in battles to keep America the land of hope and opportunity. It is the part of the world where freedom reigns and equality lives. My sincere prayer is that we always appreciate this land, its diverse citizens, and the God who reigns over us.

I am eternally grateful for the bravery of the soldiers, the explorers, the visionaries, and our forefathers who gave so much to keep the red, white, and blue flying proudly above us.

America, The Land I Love

I was born amid the lush greenery of East Tennessee where the soil produces sweetly scented flowers every summer, and ice cycles hang every winter on the rocks protruding from the earth.

I have had the privilege of traveling beyond the hills where I was born and seeing much of America. How many times have I flown from coast to coast, from north to south, and gazed at my native earth from above?

The land where majestic peaks dot the landscape as well as the deserts of the west and the green of the east. America, where flat patches of farming land form a beautiful quilt over much of the country's center. Where rivers, lakes, ponds, and oceans feed our portion of earth and glimmer in the sun as blue skies frame it all.

I have sailed in Maine, canoed in Georgia, climbed the skyscrapers of New York and the trees of North Carolina. I have seen corn growing tall in Iowa and watched the snow fall in Wyoming. I have witnessed an eagle soar on Puget Sound in Washington, and seabirds fly in Florida.

I have reached to the sky in Colorado and touched the sacred ground of fallen soldiers in Virginia. I climbed into the Grand Canyon, hiked in California, and walked through the bluegrass of Kentucky.

Oh yes, I have traveled beyond the place of my birth to states that form our union. I have crossed the country twice by car and witnessed the diversity of the land and its people. We don't have Kings or Queens, Tsars or Regimes. Our power comes from our freedom to somehow assimilate and celebrate that diversity, to form it into one strong nation.

The freedom that so many have given their lives for and still fight to maintain is where we find our unique beauty. We are not a land of old; instead we are a land where opportunity allows us to be new all the time.

Americans have seen their share of division, hatred, wars, apathy, and heartache, but somewhere in the depth of each American is a need to achieve unity, love, peace, care, and joy.

We can renew because we have the freedom to do so. We have the right to protest, protect, pray, and proceed as this great nation we call united.

Near where I was born, lies the grave of John Walker. He immigrated, as many did, from Scotland in the mid 1700s. He and his six brothers fought for our freedom in the Revolutionary War. Two brothers starved and died as prisoners of war.

Generations would follow John Walker. They lived in the hills of the east and then moved westward. They searched to find their place in the world because John and those like him won them the freedom to do so.

Besides John's grave is a tiny American Flag. He died not as a Scotsman but as an American.

This July 4th, perhaps we choose not to listen to the news about our divisiveness, but instead walk outside, touch the ground and pick up the soil. Let the grains of dirt fall through our fingers because this is our land. It is this land that will remind us to continue to pray and fight for her.

This July 4th, maybe we should turn off our phones and televisions. Perhaps, instead, we should take our children and grandchildren to visit the silent graves of fallen soldiers who gave their lives so that they could freely play in a noisy schoolyard.

This July 4th, maybe we don't need to hear political parties feuding. Instead, perhaps we need to listen to the exploding fireworks celebrating the birth of our United States.

This July 4th perhaps we should take an American Flag and

plant it in every front yard. We can dot this beautiful landscape with red, white, and blue from sea to shining sea. After all, "God did give his grace to thee."

I was born in the hills of Tennessee. In the end, I will return to the soil where the sweet, fragrant flowers grow. It is there that I will eternally rest beside my brother and the rest of my family who fought and died for the freedom they gave me to travel far.

Old Soldiers Never Die

The war in Vietnam was raging by the time the class of 1965 graduated high school. Senior boys had two choices: college or the draft. Some young men would have chosen the military anyway, draft or no draft. Many felt the call of patriotism and were proud to defend the United States, and the ideals of freedom and democracy. And many gave their lives for this dream. Way too many. The controversies surrounding the Vietnam War made this time difficult. Protest, anger, death, and politics mixed in a boiling pot, spilling over into divisiveness and apathy. Our young men came home to no fanfare or parades. They returned home, scarred both mentally and physically, to a world that forgot to say "thank you" to those who wanted only to protect and serve.

Lt. John E. Walker (1941-1998)
US Navy
circa 1965

In 1965 I headed off to college, and my brother, John Walker, who had been in the service since 1962, headed into the dark waters of North Vietnam. By August of that year, Lt. John and his entire destroyer, the USS Pritchett, were nowhere to be found. The Navy did not explain their whereabouts or mission.

Finally, after almost a year, a letter from President Lyndon Johnson was handed to my mother. The USS Pritchett had been on a secret mission traveling further into North Vietnamese waters than any other ship had ventured before. The letter let my mother know everyone on board was safe and on their way home.

During John's service in Vietnam, I received a Vietnamese doll from him. These dolls became a symbol of the war to many. She came to me in traditional dress with a straw hat that hung by a strap down her back. She moved with me wherever life took me, usually winding up safely tucked in a dresser drawer.

My brother finally arrived home in late 1966 after serving over four years in the Navy. He never discussed Nam, but his love of his comrades and the Navy never wavered.

After a diagnosis of terminal cancer in 1994, John returned to a gathering of his old shipmates on the USS Pritchett. It was there that he found the inspiration to write a history of the destroyer and present it to the US Navy.

He, along with many on the Pritchett, left this earth long before we were ready for their commissions with us to be over.

For many years during the war, I wore a POW/MIA bracelet for another warrior whose name was Major Robert Dyczkowski. These bracelets were worn by many of us to honor the fallen. They merely bore the name and rank of the soldier and the date he went missing.

When your soldier was set free, or his remains found, you were to break the metal. For me, it symbolized that the soldier was not bound any longer by shackles or life. They were found either on earth or in heaven.

My bracelet is still intact. Major Robert Dyczkowski never returned nor was ever found.

The bracelet was with my doll in that safe drawer for over

forty years. Now and then I would wonder about the Major and hope that somewhere, someway, someday those in the military who kept searching for the soldiers lost in Vietnam would find this Air Force pilot and bring him home.

When I married in 2005, my husband wanted me to have someone to help me clean our house. After a search I found Violet. Violet came to the US from Poland. She spoke perfect English, and I have loved her as part of our family for years.

One day, right before she was to arrive, my husband and I decided to create a wall of art in our dining room. Most of the paintings were his and had previously hung on various walls throughout the house. We loved the new art collection, but there was a hole that needed something else. A narrow tall space was requiring a "piece."

I ran upstairs and got the doll and the POW bracelet.

"David, why can't we put these together in a shadowbox and display them here?" I said, pointing to the odd space. "I always wanted to take these out of the drawer, and now we have the opportunity to showcase them!"

After I picked the shadowbox up from the art framer, I hung it immediately. It was perfect! The doll with the POW/MIA metal bracelet around her waist was now in an honorable place.

Violet came the following Thursday.

She was dusting in the dining room and admiring the gallery. I was getting ready for work..

"Lynn, Lynn!" she shouted.

I ran to her. She was holding the feather duster in the air as if frozen while staring at the shadowbox.

She could hardly talk, so I explained to her what the bracelet meant.

"No, no, you are not going to believe this!" She continued, "That is Robert Dyczkowski! He was found in 2001 and brought home. He is my husband's uncle. He was promoted posthumously to Colonel and is one of that last Americans from Vietnam to be buried in Arlington."

I looked at her and she at me. From Poland to America to Vietnam to Georgia to a dining room. We both stared at the doll. Tears fell down my cheeks, and I felt as if two fallen soldiers were standing there, looking at two women utterly aghast at the curious, mysterious junctions where lives meet and why. Suddenly it seemed as if the war was finally over. Peace had found two soldiers.

Memories of war and those that served never should be tucked away in a drawer. On this Memorial Day we need to remember that old soldiers never die, nor do they fade away. They should always live on in the hearts and minds of those that they served and forever honored.

The Shadowbox

Our Duty Is To Remember

This coming weekend marks the official beginning of summer. School is closing while swimming pools are opening. We are packing bags for camps and long-planned vacations. Jasmine and honeysuckle sweeten the air and gardens dot the landscape with growing vegetables, fruits, and flowers.

The beginning of summer is always a joyous event. Memorial Day weekend sparks barbeques, kids squealing in delight, and Moms and Dads everywhere enjoying a Monday holiday. However, while we laugh and play there is a soldier somewhere who is fighting on a battlefield so all of us may continue enjoying our memorial Monday.

When I pause to remember the many brave men and women who have died for me to be able to write freely, to freely wave a flag, to openly pray, to freely vote, and to be free from tyranny, I am humbled, and I need to be. We all do.

Sometimes we all act spoiled, taking for granted the freedoms we enjoy. Sometimes we are plain bratty and thankless. This weekend we might raise our flags in front of our homes while continuing a petty fight with our neighbors. We may not remember the 1.1 million American soldiers who died on the battlefield and whose fights were far from petty.

While we scream at the folks who pulled into the parking place we were waiting on at the mall, we will not remember those who screamed in pain on the beaches, in the rice paddies, the deserts, the mountains, the fields, and islands where bravery spilled over the earth. Their screams should still pierce our hearts and ring in our ears.

While we pack for our vacations to France, Belgium, the

Philippines, Panama, Italy, Germany, Mexico, the Netherlands, Vietnam, Tunisia, and the United Kingdom, we will not focus on the over 130,000 American soldiers buried in cemeteries on these foreign lands. Nor will we focus on more than 124,000 soldiers who are still missing.

While we get ready to go to Aunt June's to eat watermelon and pick summer vegetables, we will not be thinking of the Civil War battle fought on the once blood-soaked land around her house.

When we see our flag flying on this Memorial Day, are we going to remember the 50,000 soldiers who died, were maimed or wounded during the fight for our independence in the American Revolution?

During a summer evening, we will take our children to the theaters to see "Iron Man," "Thor," "Black Panther" and all those terrific fictional heroes who battle to save their people. Will we also remember to tell our children that the real heroes are those who wore the uniform of the American soldier who died for the United States and its people?

While we play with our children in the summer sun, will we think about the mother viewing the flag-draped coffin of her son or the father who died in combat before he could meet his new daughter?

Perhaps, it is right or reasonable for us to not dwell on such sadness as the fallen hero. Maybe it is right for us to laugh, love, to dispute, honk our horns, and watch "Iron Man." For it is the soldier who died and did so for us to continue to live in the land where the beginning of summer is a joyous event.

Understanding the fallen soldier is so eloquently written in this poem from long ago:

> "And when the wind in the tree-tops roared,
> The soldier asked from the deep dark grave:
> "Did the banner flutter then?"
> "Not so, my hero," the wind replied.

"The fight is done, but the banner won,
Thy comrades of old have borne it hence,
Have borne it in triumph hence."
Then the soldier spake from the deep dark grave:
"I am content."
Then he heareth the lovers laughing pass,
and the soldier asks once more:
"Are those not the voices of them that love,
That love—and remember me?"
"Not so, my hero," the lovers say,
"We are those that remember not;
For the spring has come and the earth has smiled,
And the dead must be forgot."
Then the soldier spake from the deep dark grave:
"I am content."

from "The Soldier on the Battlefield"
author unknown

It was their duty, their honor, and their courage to give. It is our duty to the fallen soldiers always to remember just who they were and why.

Let's Keep The Flag Flying

It is Memorial Day. I took a walk this morning to breathe in the fresh Georgia air and get my bit of exercise before the heat would take that outdoor option away.

I waved goodbye to my ducks that were busy eating their breakfast of cracked corn. The chipmunks were already scampering and digging. Life was as it should be as I walked through the sweet jasmine-covered arch to the street.

I needed to pull the weeds on the little piece of land we own but decided they would still be there tomorrow. Besides, pulling weeds would have disturbed the duck's breakfast! Good excuse.

The beginning of summer in the south is a joy to behold. The trees are full, spreading their leaves over lush grass. The landscape is a myriad of all the shades of green Crayola ever produced. The yards splash dots of color using flowers of purple, orange, red, pink, and yellow.

On the corner is a magnificent magnolia tree in full bloom. This year her blossoms are large and angelic white against her dark jade leaves.

I turn down the main street where golfers are playing on the course near my house. In honor of Memorial Day, the American Flag replaces the usual green and white putting green flags. The red, white, and blue against the green are striking, and I think, "What a privilege is it to be able to have a day off to play!"

I approached the top of the hill where I gazed across the rolling fields to where the Chattahoochee River bends and flows gently around our neighborhoods. The pale blue sky is teeming with marshmallow clouds that give peace to the day.

"How fortunate am I to live amid such peaceful beauty," I

thought as I continued my walk. Today my air is not filled with smoke from weaponry or exploding bombs. Fires from war do not scorch my earth. I am walking freely on the street and not hiding in fear from an enemy.

I smell the aroma of barbeque off in the distance as two birds fly above my head in a chase. I start to feel a pang of hunger and begin to drool thinking about the tomato sandwich I will have for lunch. Again, I reflect, "How grateful am I that I will not go hungry today."

I follow the same path to return home. I pass the same scenery, but then it isn't the same. There are more squirrels climbing trees, more people walking, and more flowers I didn't notice before. "God made so much that one cannot possibly see it all! How blessed am I to live where I can freely thank God for these blessings."

There are children playfully yelling in the neighborhood pool, and I remember today is the first day of their summer vacation. Studying and early hours are over for a while. I ponder, "How amazing it is that we offer every child in America an education."

I walk down my short street and notice every house has an American flag flying in the front yard. They wave in harmony as I pass. I see my little piece of land in the distance, and I realize, "How wonderful it is to be able to own a home with a backyard; weeds, ducks, chipmunks and all."

After today most folks will store their flags away until July 4th.

Perhaps we should keep the flag flying in our front yards every day.

Perhaps it will remind us that the privileges we enjoy have been given to us by the men and women who paid the ultimate price.

Wait a minute! Why don't we keep our flags flying all summer to remind us daily to be grateful for the abundance, freedom, peace, and beauty of this blessed land we call America.

The Final Flight

September 30th was a day I had looked forward to for quite a while. It had been nine months since I had seen my son. That is longer than we usually go without a visit. Colorado and Atlanta seemed to be getting further apart. It was way past time to see my boy.

Delta Flight 1817 was on time leaving Atlanta on this beautiful, warm, almost October afternoon. It felt good to sit down for a moment and unwind. I had packed a notepad, my crossword puzzles, my iPad and a few other things to keep me entertained on my flight across the country.

I love to hear the roar of the engines and see the mountains looming up to touch the clouds. I love the quilted pattern of the earth below and my silent guessing game of: "Exactly where am I?"

Flight 1817 was free from turbulent air and turbulent fliers. It was Friday and folks were on their way home from a week on business, or leaving home to visit the scenic beauty of Colorado or visit a sister, or a Dad, or a son.

I drank my diet Coke and ate my little bag of ten peanuts and settled into my journey. I thought about how hard it is when your children live far away. How hard it is to be a mom and have to let go of those precious ones and let them have their lives.

Is that fact in a guidebook about children? Yes, they grow up and can move away! Oh well, I am just fortunate enough to be on this flight to cure the distance part of motherhood.

Finally, the jet engines started to slow down, and I knew we were preparing for our descent into Denver. I was looking forward to seeing those crazy looking Cirque du Soleil tents looming on the flat plains outside of the city.

I just described the Denver International Airport. The white fiberglass peaks are supposed to emulate the Rocky Mountains, but I have yet to get that visual. It doesn't matter; they are a welcome sight for this old mama who just wants to see her 41-year-old baby boy.

The plane landed smoothly and started to taxi toward the gate. My watch said we were ten minutes early. Yippee!!

"Ladies and Gentlemen, this is your captain speaking. Today we have a fallen soldier who has traveled home with us. I will ask you to remain seated until we have returned him safely back to his family. He is escorted today by a Marine Captain. Please stay seated until we tell you it is ok to de-board."

The Marine Captain stood up in front of the plane, his back to all of us. When he saluted the pilot, two hundred plus fliers loudly applauded. He then descended to the ground below.

Directly to my right, I could see the activity on the tarmac. Black SUV's pulled up next to the plane. Marines in full dress uniforms filed out and stood in formation. Then a hearse and a Honda pulled up.

While the passengers looked out the windows, complete and utter silence enveloped the interior as well as the exterior of Delta flight 1817.

A tall young man accompanied his father out of the Honda, holding him as he stood. A mother was being held tightly by a friend or family member. Another young woman stood alone.

I could see every emotion in their bodies and faces. As the cargo hold door opened, the father started to crumble. His arms folded around his head as if to block out what his brain was not prepared to see.

The mother was grasping her friend tighter, as she too, started to fall.

The Military honor guard in perfect splendor and cadence lifted the flag-draped silver coffin from the plane and marched it toward the hearse with the red, white, and blue flag crisply covering the fallen Marine. This flag would never fly again above our land, but instead, be folded and given to the family now watching their son departing from his final flight.

A soldier who fought for us to be able to fly anywhere we desire came home to Colorado on an almost October day. He fought and died for us to have the freedom to sit down when his flag rises or to respectfully stand. A soldier whose bravery keeps us having the freedom to make choices and share differing beliefs. A soldier who enabled us to fight our political battles and vote for our leaders.

A young soldier who took his last flight for us to fly free. A soldier whose parents didn't get to say goodbye or have a chance to revisit their baby boy.

Finally, the hearse drove away, along with the Honda and the Marines in their black SUV.

What remained were passengers with tears in their eyes, some even sobbing. When we left the plane, there was not a word spoken by a single passenger as we walked back toward our own lives.

I spent five blissful days with my son. I went for walks with him daily. I watched as he ran in front of me to play with his dog in the park near a school. He threw the ball as Miner chased it into the field. I watched as my son's legs moved and his arms flew into the air. I watched his mouth form into laughter and his voice boom as he called the dog's name. I absorbed every moment of this picture of living while knowing another mother would never have another new image.

I silently prayed, and as I did, I saw the American flag in the schoolyard.

Thanks to the fallen soldier, the red, white, and blue was still flying high against the cloudless, sundrenched Colorado sky.

The Land Below The Red, White, And Blue

When I pass a flag with those stars and stripes flying above me, I momentarily lose the news of the day, the political rhetoric, and the divisiveness. There is a swelling of pride and a reminder of how fortunate I was to be born in the land below the flag.

I probably need to place an American flag in my kitchen to calm me down when I get angry with politicians who act as if they have forgotten where they live. I should fly the banner above the television to keep me from shouting obscenities at the screen when the news makes it seem there is nothing good to report about our country.

When the red, white, and blue drapes a soldier's coffin my heart leaps for the many who have died so that our flag can continue to wave in the air over a free land. When the flag is hoisted above a school ground, or over a library, or atop a government building I remind myself of the privileges that enable all of us to go to school, learn to read any book we choose and to freely elect or reject our leaders.

The American flag flying at half mast brings tears to my eyes because those who we deemed great are gone, or tragedy has brought our citizens to their collective knees.

The flag of America is a symbol of our hope, unification, spirit, and glory. To gain our independence was a task deemed impossible by many of our ancestors in the mid-1700s. Bravery, intelligence, courage, and conviction turned an impossibility into the United States of America. From 1776 until today we have defended the right to stay united and free.

Most of us were alive in 2001 when terrorists attacked our nation. We shed tears of disbelief, but we were united in grief. We forgot we were Democrats or Republicans with differences because we remembered to shout, "This is OUR country, OUR flag, and we will defend it!" We ran outside and put up the red, white, and blue above our porches and in our yards because we who mourned were all Americans.

When we argue over guns, over immigration, taxes, healthcare, or over which candidate is the best, we must pause for a moment and be grateful we can debate, disagree, and sometimes behave like morons because we are free to open our mouths.

When we attend church and gather around a Sunday School water cooler to discuss what is wrong with our country, why not stop to give thanks to God for placing us in a land where we are free to worship, free to sing of glory, free to ask for forgiveness, and freely praise God and not a dictator.

This July 4th, while the grill is heating and we slice the watermelon, why not pause for a moment to celebrate the very fact that we have food to eat and most of our children know no hunger. While the kids swim in the sun and play among the shade trees, let's remind ourselves of the children who walk miles to escape violence and those who will die along the way.

If we cut our finger while slicing the watermelon, let's stop and remember we will probably not die because a "Doc in the box" is within a mile and available when we do dumb things like slice our finger. We do not have to travel miles or walk along a dirt path searching for help.

As the fireworks explode into the night sky and cascade to the ground in vibrant colors, let's pause to think about the soldier who hears bombs explode on the battlefield and watches as a comrade falls to the ground. We must all remember those who have paid the price with their lives so that we may fly our beautiful flag.

If I could, I wish I could bring folks around our country together for one big July 4th picnic. I would ask all of America to join hands and give thanks to God for this great country we all call home and pray that He continues to let the red, white, and blue fly proudly above us.

Celebrate

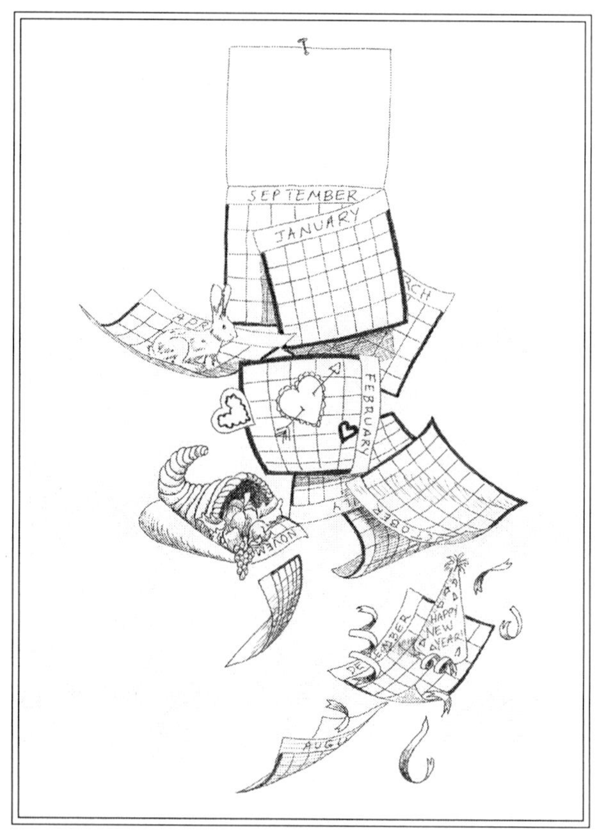

There is hardly a month on the calendar which does not denote a day to celebrate something. From New Year's Day to New Year's Eve, we have days marked for celebration.

We all enjoy a holiday when we have a chance to gather for a party, honor someone, send a gift of love, hunt eggs, wave flags, dress in costumes, and then give thanks for it all.

These specially marked days put a pause on routine and a skip in our step. They provide us with laughter, hugs, and memories throughout all the months of our lives, giving us a cause to celebrate!

Skip Resolutions, Get A Bucket

All my family has left the building. Everybody has gone home to Florida and Colorado to start another year. All of us need to lose the cookie weight, pack up Christmas, and to go back to work and school. Some will make resolutions. I will declare I will not cry next time they leave, but I always do.

Most New Year's resolutions are not long lasting. Go to the gym and see how many folks are there January 4 and then check again on March 4. Where did all those resolute people go?

There just might be a solution to keeping a resolution through an amazing, surreal story of my own.

Start out by buying a bucket or get one out of the garage. It can be tiny, or its handle can even be missing. It does not matter. But, what does matter is it must not be used for anything else. It is your bucket with your name on it.

In July 2015, my friend Ricki was preparing to turn another significant year older. She was not handling it well. The ordinarily vivacious Ricki was somber and quiet, so unlike her. Two other friends and I decided to give her a surprise birthday party.

Since the day I met her ten years ago Ricki has always had a "Bucket List." A journey to there, to read this or that, to volunteer, or to improve her golf game. Once she retired from being a school counselor, the buckets kept stacking up because, by gosh, she was emptying them. Amazing!

Personally, I never had a bucket list. Most of my life was spent working and supporting my children. As a single mother, my dreams were merely putting food on the table and paying the bills. If I got through the month without a big scare, I was a happy person.

When I met Ricki, I had just married after twenty years on my own. My children were grown and educated. I figured as long as my kids got an education and were safe, anything afterward was just gravy.

We decided to use all sizes of pink buckets as decor for the party. They hung from ribbons on the chandelier in the dining room and over the island in the kitchen. Buckets held utensils, napkins, and party favors. As the ladies arrived, we instructed them to write an anonymous bucket list item and throw it in the pink bucket in the foyer. To say Ricki was surprised and her spirit lifted was an understatement!

And then, after dinner, we settled down to play a funny, original game. I reached into the bucket list bucket, pulled out the slips of paper, and read what each guest had written. The rest tried to guess which lady wanted to achieve that particular dream. Some were so funny that it brought howls of laughter. Some were serious, and many wanted to travel to far away locations.

About halfway through I realized I had not written down my own bucket list item. I grabbed a piece of paper, started to write one thing, quickly changed it and then threw the paper into the bucket.

That was my very first bucket list item.

Long ago, as a college freshman, I started writing. A professor begged me to change my major and go into journalism. Of course, I didn't listen. For the next forty years, somewhere in my soul was this nagging or longing to write.

I would submit articles occasionally, and to my surprise, they were often published. But, because I needed to put food on the table, the writing dream was always on the back burner waiting for a day to come to a boil.

Around the time of Ricki's party, when I went to bed each night, I would feel a tug to write a story about my incredible high school class. One morning, I promised God I would. I did, then sent it to my hometown newspaper and they published it.

Three months after Ricki's party, I became a weekly columnist for the same paper.

My bucket list item, written and thrown in a bucket in July was, "I would like to be a newspaper columnist."

Something ingrained in the recesses of my mind made me quickly put a long-held dream on paper and throw it in a bright pink bucket.

This January 1st, reach deep into your soul and find God's bucket list item for you. It is there. Write it down, place in your bucket and you might be surprised at how quickly that bucket might empty.

Sometimes we lose resolutions, but we find God's will for us if only we believe in the dream.

Happy New Year!

Mama And Her Chocolate Box Of Valentines

When Valentine's Day is over, we will have written our names on cards under the word love, and moved on toward the next day. The cards will be tossed or possibly saved if one is exceptional. Some tender hearts will keep them all and reflect on a day when someone cared enough to send Hallmark.

My mother left me a Whitman's Sampler chocolate box from the 1950s. The chocolate is long gone but what remains inside the box is a treasure trove of memories. She had saved all her Valentines from her childhood. There must be more than one hundred cards which were signed in the early 1920s in that yellow box. Some are decorated intricately with lace and art while others are cute, cherub faces riding horses and holding bouquets of roses.

They are signed by friends and family which include Madge, Virginia, Lester, Helen, Mary Ruth, Junior, and James Robbins. I believe my mother and James Robbins wound up having a special relationship at one time, but then Mama fell for Daddy and James became romantic history.

We buried Mama in Monterey, Tennessee on July 1, 2010. Ironically, it was also my Dad's birthday. We all knew Daddy got a mighty fine present that day in heaven.

I was standing near the front porch of the funeral home where we were to have the service. The bright sunshine mixed with crisp mountain air refreshed my soul. The perfect day for Mama to be laid to rest beside Daddy in the little town where she was born.

A man approached me, took my hand tenderly and said,

"Lynn, I am James Robbins, an old friend of your mother's. She was an extraordinary lady."

I covered my other hand with his and whispered, "I know who you are, Mr. Robbins, and she thought you special too."

I think I would have made Mama proud by my reply to him.

James died two years later at the age of ninety-two. His little cards that he wrote to her when he was five are still in the chocolate box.

I am in awe of those who marry and stay together until they depart this earth. They are held together like the old glue used on those cards. They forge memories, and their lives intertwine into one. They have braved the harsh elements of marriage and love. They make it work.

I was fortunate to be raised by parents who did truly love one another. Did they hurt each other? Sure. Don't we all. But, did the love survive? Until the day they died.

Love is a complicated component in our lives. Love can break you or make you. There are all different types and all different ways to show appreciation and respect for another.

I have known so many broken by love. Couples who fell in love and lost. The resentment and heartache left them unable to love again out of the sheer fear of losing. For them, love became a problem instead of a blessing.

I can understand that. A broken heart has no medicine for the pain. It is slow to heal, and when it does, there will still be scars which can act up at times. Broken hearts can cause a fractured soul and can make you sicker than you ever thought you could be.

The best cure for a broken heart is the very thing that broke it—love.

Many people are content to live without a mate. However, they still love. They love God, their family, friends, and they love life. If they ever did have a broken heart, they have turned the corner and enjoyed what is now in their lives entirely.

I know one thing for sure, when I look back on it, I met

some beautiful people while giving my heart away to them. I wouldn't take anything for that.

Many years after our divorce, my first husband met a beautiful woman who makes him happy which makes me happy. We were young when we married, and we were still young when we waved goodbye.

It would be twenty years before I married again, but I did find love a time or two along the way and lost it as well. I have stayed friends with some who broke my heart only because they were worth it. I believe that is love in its finest form.

I am grateful for the few scars on my heart. I feel compassion and have learned we should never take for granted any love. I am compelled to reach out to others and tell them broken hearts do heal, and love can continue in a thousand ways.

We carry lost love with us always. It is important not to continue to cry, but to smile at its best memories. James Robbins did just that 85 years after sending an extraordinary lady her first Valentine.

A Forgetful Daughter's Sunday Walk

Last week was one of those weeks when Sunday went to Sunday in two days. I don't know what happened! Every day just seemed to be packed with "get 'to do's' done," "'don't forget' memos," and "got to get in exercises."

I took a quick trip to LaGrange to meet with my sweet editor, Jennifer, and have lunch. Hurry, hurry, and hurry was the rule of the week. I did not even have time to run by the old house, call on friends, or buy shoes at Solomon's in my favorite town. Now, that's bad!

By Sunday morning I was exhausted. I woke up, drank my coffee, and decided to take a long walk.

On many occasions when I take walks alone, I try to contemplate the subject and words for my next column. Often, I commune with God, say a prayer, and ask for inspiration. Those walks seem to clear my head and get me headed in a better direction.

It was a beautiful Sunday morning. The sky was clear blue and seemed to be higher than usual. The streaks of clouds mixed with vapor trails from the jets I could see as the sun glinted off their shiny metal. The cool air was warming with each step, and I kept looking to make sure God was somewhere around to help me come up with an idea for a story.

I approached the perfect dogwood tree blooming and looming upward to the sky. It was full of blossoms which looked whiter than most. The tree stood proudly among the new greenery of oaks, pines, and maples. Where the other dogwoods were slowly losing a bit of their luster, this one was as if it dared itself to drop even one petal.

I couldn't help but walk toward it. I pulled one of the branches down to study the flowers.

"Yes, it does look like a cross with a crown of thorns in the middle. There is the blood of the Lord on each petal which is so thin that I can't believe this stays on a branch!" I said to myself as I remembered the legend of the dogwood tree.

"Lynn, what is today?" I heard a voice within my soul speaking as if I were not very smart.

"Huh?" I thought.

Then as if the dogwood fell on my head, I remembered it was Palm Sunday! And, no I wasn't in church, and yes, you are right, I needed the dogwood to fall on my head!

How could I forget it was Palm Sunday?! As I contemplated this, I took the little flower in my hand and thought about the Lord's week long ago consumed with terror, heartache, abuse, injustice, betrayal, and ultimately, victory. By contrast, my week was just busy.

In my busyness, I forgot that this was the beginning of Holy Week. A week that begins with praise for Jesus as he walks down a path on Sunday and by the following Friday, He is walking down a road filled with people cheering for His crucifixion.

I broke off a little twig with a dogwood flower and held it in my hand as I continued my long walk. The flower was so fragile and beautiful. I touched the stain of reddish brown on each petal and felt sadness as my finger passed over the thorny green in the middle of the blossom. I felt joy when I saw tiny, new, green leaves supporting the flower.

The whole story of Holy week is in the little flower of the dogwood tree. Life, death, and renewal. The Lord was a beautiful gift from God and the cross the petals form is a lovely reminder.

As I continued my shameful walk, I again looked up to heaven.

"Father, I apologize for being so busy with my week that I

forgot about yours. Please, forgive me."

With the little blossom in my hand, I keenly noticed the radiant colors of the earth. The green canopy of trees gently swayed as if they were keeping a beat to a song I couldn't hear.

Memories flooded my soul as I thought about past Easters with grandparents, children, cousins, and my parents. Egg hunts, dinners, baskets, flowers, and church services consumed our day.

"Wait, my parents!" I suddenly thought. "What day is today?!"

Not only was it Palm Sunday, but it was April 9th, my parent's anniversary. They were married after church services on an Easter Sunday in 1939. Today I am comforted they are together again beyond the blue sky.

WOW!! Am I glad I went on this walk! I might have forgotten Christmas if I hadn't!

Sometimes when we get too busy or too forgetful (because we are), we should take a walk with God. He will slow us down to look at the infinite sky, the radiant earth, and the blossoming dogwood tree.

He will show us how we are so important to Him that He took the time out of His week to lay down His life for us.

He will also show us the road to redemption, forgiveness, and understanding because He sincerely loves us even if we sometimes do forget important things.

He will even give us a gift when we least expect it; like a story to write.

Happy Easter to all, notice the dogwoods and have a nice walk.

This Mother's Day I Shall Wear Red

I vividly recall being in church on Mother's Day and straining to see who was wearing a white or a red carnation corsage. I was incredibly grateful my mom was beside me with red flowers pinned to her dress. Life without my grandmother and mom was too horrific to ponder. I remember the extreme sadness I felt as a ten-year-old when I saw the white carnations others wore on those May Sundays when spring was abundant with life.

White carnations were Anna Jarvis's mother's favorite flower. After her beloved mother died, Anna started to petition for a holiday honoring mothers in the early 1900s. She chose the white carnation in honor of the mother she missed so much. The red carnation later symbolized love and respect for the mothers who still were living.

I was twenty-three and standing beside my grandmother when she first wore a white corsage to honor my great-grandmother on Mother's Day in 1971. I witnessed a tear fall from her eyes as I tried to combat the stinging behind mine. I realized no matter at what age we lose our mothers, our eyes will brim with tears, and our hearts mourn when our mother no longer sits beside us on that special Sunday morning in May.

It has taken me longer than I anticipated to remember my mother as she was before her last year on earth. I watched this beautiful woman slowly decline from vibrancy to death every day for twelve months.

After she died, I couldn't erase the image of her last year nor the sadness within my heart. I tried in vain to visualize my mom in her younger days when she would get tickled over something silly we did, or drive a golf ball perfectly straight down the middle of a fairway on every attempt. I longed to detect the sweet aroma of the apple pie she baked and taste the chicken only she knew how to fry. I prayed to remember the lady who would spend a day shopping with me for school clothes or the mother who would surprise me with a dress exquisitely created by her skill on the sewing machine.

I wanted to hear the voice she would use to calm me down or teach me a lesson with her amazing wisdom and grace. However, all I could see was the frail woman who held onto my hand in her last hour. In my mind, the pain she endured in dying seemed to have replaced the exuberance she embodied in living.

I would study a photograph of her when she was in her thirties as if I was trying to recall who she was. I began to pray earnestly, "Please God, take the image of mom's difficult last days away and replace it with the sweet memories of her youth, strength, and beauty."

This June it will be eight years since my mother passed away. My prayers weren't answered immediately but instead revealed to me slowly in very unusual ways. One was in a dream.

I dreamed I was walking beside a water's edge with a clean, sandy shoreline. The water lapped onto my bare feet as the falling sun caused the sky to turn rose and the calm water to sparkle. In the distance I noticed a woman strolling toward me. A gentle breeze caused her pale dress to flow around her bare sun-kissed legs just below the knees. As I moved closer to her, I realized it was my mother, and I started to run. Before I reached her outstretched arms, I awoke to the morning sun.

When I walked into our kitchen to grab my coffee, my husband noticed I was humming a tune. "What is the name of that song?" he questioned.

I suddenly realized I was humming an old gospel tune I heard many times in my grandparent's Baptist church as a young girl:

"There's a land that is fairer than day,
And by faith we can see it afar;
For the Father waits over the way
To prepare us a dwelling place there.
In the sweet by and by,
We shall meet on that beautiful shore."

I no longer recall mother in the sad days of her life ending, but in the glorious days when she created art with a needle, when the aroma of sweet desserts wafted from her kitchen, and when she filled our home with love. Gratefully, today I only see her youthful, spirited soul walking to greet me on that beautiful shore.

This Mother's Day I shall wear red because my mother's love never left and still fills my heart with joy and a sweet heavenly song.

Elizabeth & John Walker
circa 1941

Thankful For Falling Leaves

Most Monday mornings I head to my office with my cup of wake-up coffee to start my column. Usually, a theme has been percolating in my mind all week, so when I type the first sentence, the words begin to pour onto the page.

Today, I sit at my desk with my same coffee cup and all I can think of is, "Why is my neighbor's leaf blower so loud?!" My percolating brain has been on the fritz all week. My mind has centered around getting ready for the holidays. Menus, wrapping, decorating, and gift ideas have left little room for column thought.

I call my "go to partner" for help. "God, what do you want me to write about this week? Got any ideas?"

Again, silence, except for the leaf blower. I glance out my window to check how much longer I must contend with the noise when a flurry of leaves falls past my window in a shower of orange and gold.

In the 1950s most folks owned a stereo housed in a piece of furniture called a console. Our house was no exception. My Dad loved to play albums while whistling along with the music.

Johnny Mercer wrote the English lyrics to a French song from the 1940s called "Autumn Leaves." The song was recorded by many in the years to follow. To this day, when leaves start to fall, I find myself humming its tune.

Even as I child, this song made me sad. I wasn't sure exactly what it meant, but I knew it was about loss.

"Daddy, why do you play that old sad song all the time?" I would question. "Isn't it about losing someone important?"

"Well, it depends on how you look at it. You hear the loss, and I hear the love," he would answer.

Most all of us have experienced love and loss. Whether these losses were caused by death, illness, rejection, or by just waving a painful goodbye, it was still a heartbreak. Our grief hurts and is debilitating. We endure sleepless nights and long, sad days.

There will be someone reading this today who is facing the holidays with enormous trepidation because of grief. Many will sit at a Thanksgiving table with one less person in November.

They are wondering how they can get through today, much less the holidays. Many will say, "There is not much to be thankful for this season."

I have a friend who has endured many losses in life. Both her husband and daughter are gone. Yet, when I see her face, it is joyful. She honors their memory with her attitude and faith. God shines through her like a beacon. Her tragedy has inspired others to heal and regain hope.

Yes, there are times I grieve for loved ones I have lost, but what a gift they were to my life. To experience love, to experience sharing a deep connection to another, and to have their existence cross my path is a reason to be very thankful.

When I think of their love, I long to see them again. I long to have them be as they were; a part of my holidays, a part of my life.

However, am I happy they once were a part? You bet! I have found that losing is often a recipe for appreciation. I would not take anything for the love that God gave me to share with them. It is their love and my loss that made me stronger, brought me closer to God and taught me how to lend a helping hand to a heartbroken friend. It was that pain that made me empathetic to others and made me write words which form sentences to share with you.

The loss of family and friends has made me appreciate those still on life's journey with me. I am more aware of how precious and fragile life is and how each person in my life is a gift.

This Thanksgiving we all need to look at the folks who are at our table and appreciate the love we share. We need to be thankful for a merciful God who aids us through tragedy and reminds us no loss is ever truly final.

In my memory, I see a Thanksgiving table filled with family; I smell the roses an old boyfriend once gave me, and hear my father whistling a tune as the stereo plays on. I choose not to recall the pain of their loss; I instead want to remember their love.

The leaf blower has gone silent, and I smile as I watch the autumn leaves drift by my window.

Thanksgiving In The Garden

The turkey is golden, the casseroles are in the oven, and the pies are cooling on the counter. The family is in the living room, and the noise is accelerating as their hunger deepens.

The screeching sound of children and the adults' laughter rolls through the house the same way the scent of roasted turkey wafts its way through rooms.

The sweet potato soufflé and I have a quiet moment as I watch the marshmallows transition into pale shades of gold inside the oven. As I do, I catch a glimpse of myself in the glass.

I see a reflection which is a blend of my parents' features. My eyes are my father's, and his father's, and my great grandfather's. These eyes captured in the reflection represent over a century of family ties.

It is the year 2000, the first Thanksgiving without my father. I am not counting Thanksgiving 1999 because I believe he still joined us at the table that memorable day.

On November 22, 1999, Ray Caraway Walker left this earth. He passed peacefully, gratefully, and humbly into the arms of angels. He was 85, married to mother for 60 years and had survived the death of his son by 18 months.

We took my Dad home from Georgia to be laid to rest on a barren hillside in the mountains of Tennessee where names of those he knew and loved, including his only son, are etched in granite sprung from the ground.

There were many things my father adored in life: golf, hardwood trees, pecan pie, and my mother. Not necessarily in that order, except for maybe, the golf. Mom was never too sure about whether my father loved her, or golf, more!

His service was on November 24th, the day before Thanksgiving. He had wanted it to be brief and by the gravesite only. However, a cold wind whirled in the mountains that day, so we held a little service in the chapel of the funeral home my cousin owned.

None of us was prepared to have a formal funeral, so I quickly wrote a eulogy and told the Cate sisters to play the piano and sing. Mary and Elaine Cate were the daughters of my parents' childhood friends. Both were talented musicians who had no problem jumping to the task at hand.

"Anything specific you want us to play?" Elaine asked.

After a brief pause, I responded, "'The Tennessee Waltz'."

The girls looked puzzled. Mom stoically glanced at me and then a slight smile lit her grieving face.

"Well, Dad loved music. He loved to whistle a tune, and it was usually the 'Tennessee Waltz.' It was his favorite!" I stated.

The song was played sweetly on the piano. Afterward, Elaine put her hands on the keyboard as Mary softly sang an old hymn, "In the Garden."

My mother took my hand. "In the Garden" was Dad's mother's favorite song. Throughout his life, whenever he heard the hymn, a tear would cascade down his cheek. The Cate sisters chose it randomly without any idea how special it was for all of us. I love how God often reminds us that life does continue and you will see your loved ones again, possibly in a garden somewhere.

The following day was Thanksgiving. Our family, who had gathered to say goodbye to my father would, once again, scatter to other parts of the country.

However, it was Thanksgiving. Why not, before we say our goodbyes, gather for a meal? "Where?" was the one-word unified answer.

There is a chain of restaurants originating in Tennessee correctly named The Cracker Barrel. They promote down-home country cooking, sell old-time candies and hometown gifts.

They might be open on this holiday.

"Do they ever close?" one of the kids asked.

As the group walked through the doors, eyes widened to take us all in.

A sweet lady with the same Tennessee twang I have escorted us to the largest round table Cracker Barrel owned. There was no golden turkey on a platter as the centerpiece, but they were serving the bird with all the "fixins."

We started telling stories about how Daddy would sneak into the kitchen so Mama wouldn't spot him and steal deviled eggs. Then when he sat at the table and ate more, he would wink at all of us when Mama wasn't looking.

Stories continued about my humorous father and his good old horse sense. Stories of family times shared and the losses experienced. Stories spun around the table as the wind whirled around the mountain. Stories that warmed our spirits and dried our eyes.

In the Tennessee Cracker Barrel that day, I realized I was watching the ever-changing face of a family. As in all families, members come and go, and our mighty patriarch was gone.

"Can I interest you in some dessert?" The waitress interrupted my thoughts.

She continued, "We have pumpkin and apple pie with ice cream, but my favorite is the pecan pie!"

We all smiled, glancing at one other.

"Oh, I will have the pecan pie!" we shouted at the same time.

Laughter filled the table because we all knew that Daddy was sitting among us that Thanksgiving day, enjoying one last piece of his favorite dessert before disappearing behind the pearly gates.

I took the sweet potato soufflé to the table where anxious faces were waiting. One of my daughters sat directly across from me with her long blond hair framing her face. Her eyes met mine.

The eyes were the same as those reflected in the oven door. Those eyes which graced century-old photos and a father's face.

As her eyes gazed into mine, I could swear I saw Dad sitting at a table in the garden, having a piece of pecan pie with his family, while the Tennessee Waltz softly played in the background.

Thank you, God, for the eternal gift of family.

L to R: unknown, unknown,
Ray Walker, Robert Walker
circa 1970

Joy

Christmas has always been my favorite holiday! I celebrate the blessing of Christ's birth with gusto, glitter, and giving.

Folks laugh when I announce, "It's July, we need to think about Christmas!" Christmas puts a song in our hearts and joy in our souls. What is there not to love about Christmas?

As long as I live, I will remain as a child during the holidays. I will gaze at the stars with wonder, decorate a birthday cake for the baby born on a magical night long ago, and rejoice with the loves of my life.

Joy to the World!

Finding The Joy Of Christmas

It was the beginning of December, and it was time to hang my old Christmas wreaths on my windows and front door. Once finished I decided they looked just too tired and bland. What could I do to make these wreaths come alive?

I traveled to Hobby Lobby to look for ideas and found the perfect one! Three letters in glittering gold, JOY. I took my find home and hung the word with red and gold ribbon on my dull wreaths. The sun caught the glittering word, and, by gosh, those wreaths became downright "joyful!"

Christmas is about God, family, friends, and laughter. It is about children, make-believe, and sugar cookies. It is about ribbon, wreaths and wrapping paper. Christmas is about giving to those we love and to those we might never meet. Christmas joy is found when it is given away.

Long ago, while in a high school, Tina was a seventeen-year-old girl who wore a beautiful coat which many of her friends admired. The camel hair and lamb's wool wrap was an extravagant gift from her usually frugal mother. The subtle heather plaid wool with its luxurious chocolate fur lining made the coat so unique, it became a treasure that kept Tina's soul and body always warm.

One day, Tina heard a story about a younger girl who attended her same school. Even though Tina didn't personally know the young girl, her story weighed heavily on Tina's heart.

Fourteen-year-old Sara had lost her mother, leaving her to care for her alcoholic father as well as a younger brother. To say there was much weight on Sara's slim shoulders would be an understatement.

Sara was a pretty girl with long blond hair and a face like an angel. She was too young to seek actual employment, but she earned income by babysitting and doing odd jobs around her neighborhood. She desperately needed a winter coat, and for months she saved her dollars and change to buy the most modest jacket she could afford.

The winter winds were picking up, and Sara layered herself in sweaters to go to school. Finally, she thought excitedly, "This weekend, I will buy my jacket, and pray I have enough money!"

Once Saturday arrived she excitedly went to the old cabinet in the hallway to retrieve the money she had safely hidden in a tin can. When she opened the cabinet door, she saw the can was gone, along with every cent of her hard-earned cash. She searched and searched the shelves as hot tears started to sting her face as the truth dawned on her; her money had been stolen.

Right then, Sara knew her Daddy had found her savings and she knew what he used it for. And, sadly, she was right. Around the corner, she saw he had passed out in the old chair in the living room, and empty liquor bottles were strewn across the floor.

Upon hearing Sara's story, Tina slid her beautiful, extravagant coat off her shoulders. The cold air was stinging her bare skin as she handed it to a friend who lived close to Sara. "Please, put this in a beautiful box, and place it on Sara's porch on Christmas morning without a note as to where it came from," she instructed her friend.

"Won't your mother be upset that you are doing this?" her friend asked.

"Maybe for a bit, but I think she will understand. You see, her buying me the coat made us happy, but me giving it away will give us "joy."

Sara never knew who gave her the mysterious package she found wrapped in red flocked paper topped with a huge white bow on that Christmas morning. However, when she placed the coat across her shoulders, the fur warmed her, and joy filled her heart.

Tina was standing near her locker when school resumed after Christmas. She saw Sara walk through the door wearing the luxurious coat while a broad smile lit her angelic face. As Tina hung her new very inexpensive jacket in her locker, she laughed because she now understood the true richness of Christmas joy.

My Christmas wreaths became new by adding the gold glitter of joy. For those of you who think Christmas is too commercialized, too tiring, too much trouble, and can't wait for it to be over, try finding your own joy and then give it away to someone who needs it. Your Christmas will be alive and new again just like my wreaths and the spirit of two teenage girls from long ago.

Christmas is Christmas because an Angel appeared and said, "Behold I bring you good tidings of Great Joy!" What a wonderful word.

***Part of this true story was the first essay I wrote in college. I promised my professor I would try to get it published one day. I dedicate this to the memory of Dr. Fred Freeman, LaGrange College, LaGrange, Georgia and for his belief that one day I would do just that.**

Opening The Door To The Season

I transform my home into my winter wonderland every December. The illuminated Christmas village spreads over the top of the dining room buffet. The snow has fallen on the mirrored lake, and the church steeple rises high above the houses. The children are playing, the dogs are barking, the moms are shopping, and the ceramic Santa is waiting around the corner to deliver his bounty on Christmas morning.

The Snow Village is one of my favorite Christmas decorations. It reminds me of an idyllic movie scene I produce only in my mind. When I gaze into the little houses and buildings topped with fallen snow, I wish I could travel there and stay a while.

A three-foot Santa awaits you at the end of our foyer. His robe, handmade from old quilts, is a patchwork beauty and he is holding a lighted Christmas tree. He was a gift from friends who I worked with long ago. I adore Santa's happy face and old-time charm, and I still love the friends who knew I would.

The big nine-foot tree with unique ornaments and finery adorns the living room. The wrapped presents are ready to go under its branches awaiting a paper eruption on Christmas morn.

The mantle holds holly, twigs of green and sprigs of cotton. Large candles sit at each corner and a wooden board which reads "Let it Snow" hangs underneath the mantle. The sign was a gift from my dear friend who loves the snow, Christmas, and family gatherings as much as I do.

There is another tree which sits on a side table in the breakfast room. It is a skinny four-foot pencil called "David's Tree," and it has a story of its own. This tree is not pretty, yet, it is extraordinary.

Six years ago, my husband David and I needed to be in separate locales for Christmas. His mother was coming from New Orleans for a visit and his grown children were coming as well. I was in Florida with other family members because of my daughter's illness. Often combined families have to make difficult choices, and this was one.

David decided before I left not to put up the big tree or many decorations. We did not have enough time, nor did I have enough energy and spirit.

When I gazed at my spiritless house, I just couldn't leave it that way. One day, when he was away on a business trip, I bought the little tree and a few ornaments I thought he would enjoy. Since he loves fishing, golf, photography, his hometown of New Orleans, pizza, and the beach, I adorned the tree with trimmings representing those items.

Not many trees have red and white fishing floats and a slice of glass pizza hanging from their branches, but this one sure does. Along with old colored lights are beach chairs, a camera, golfers, and a replica of a po' boy sandwich.

Everything David loved was hanging on the tree when he arrived home. I don't think I ever gave him anything he appreciated more.

We add another crazy decoration to the thin pine every year. However, on the back of the tree hangs a beautiful pink ornament which is a reminder of the reason there is "David's Tree" and the daughter who was fighting cancer on Christmas in 2011.

As you walk through the kitchen, there are utensils held in a snowman container. Easels hold Christmas platters on bookshelves. Fragrant evergreen candles fill the air. Soon, the scent of cookies made by my granddaughter and me will waft through the rooms.

On the table in the foyer, is the Nativity and the reason for the other decorations that adorn the house. The stable is straw-covered, and the wise men are walking toward the Christ child. An angel is watching over them while the lambs and cows are settling down to rest on a bed of raffia. The shepherds are standing still, filled with awe and wonder as they gaze upon the miracle child.

I realize upon finishing my decorating, that I don't need to travel to an idyllic setting for Christmas. There may not be snow on my roof, but there will be laughter and joy rising as high as a church steeple. There will be chaos and messes, so it will not look perfect. The dogs will bark too loudly, the children will play rowdily, and the family will gather to tell the miracle born in the stable on the first Christmas day, "Thank you."

Christmas is not in the décor, nor is it the presents we buy. It is in the love of friends and family. It is our spirit that reveals the wonder of Christmas and the love of the Christ child that makes the holiday perfect year after year.

Enjoy putting a wreath on your front door and invite the wonder of Christmas inside.

"But Mama, It's Christmas!"

I was born on September 27, exactly nine months and two days after Christmas. I was also born with a birthmark on my left shoulder that was an exact three-inch replica of a Christmas tree in a pot.

"You have a Christmas tree on your arm!" the kids would shout as I jumped into a pool or played in a sleeveless shirt. I was proud of my unusual birthmark because no one on this earth loved Christmas more than I.

My mother hoped my obsession with December 25th might wane as I grew older. When young, I would get so excited during the holidays I would have an asthma attack or break out in a crazy rash, making the holidays a bit difficult for her.

"Lynn, come in from the cold! You are going to make yourself sicker!" she would shout from the front door.

"But, Mama, it's Christmas!" I would yell back as if the holiday would save me from myself.

Much to her dismay, I just wheezed and itched my way through the cold, praying for snow. I would gaze into a gray winter sky looking for Rudolph's red nose and heavenly angels turning gloom to glory.

I was despondent when the birthmark faded away after many years. I outgrew asthma, the rashes finally subsided, and Mama went to be with those heavenly angels that turned her life into glory.

The years flew by and brought children, grandchildren, joy, sadness, successes, and failures. However, nothing changed my love and excitement for Christmas.

It is the holiday that brings out the best in folks. Now, there are a lot of "Bah Humbugs" out there who say it is too commercial, too busy, too chaotic, and too expensive. However, I believe Christmas is what each person makes it to be.

My grandmother was not a rich woman, but she made the richest jam cakes every Christmas to give to her friends and family. Cameron, who lives down the street, makes little pumpkin loaves of bread to give to all our neighbors. Our Bunko group has a party every year, and instead of giving gifts we donate money to several charities.

It is the season when the churches are fuller, the lights are brighter, the air more expectant, and folks more giving. What is there not to love about Christmas?

I walked into Hobby Lobby on a hot July day in Georgia, and they were putting Christmas ornaments on shelves. People were aghast at the sight! July?!

Not me. The hair on my arms lifted as if a cold winter chill had seeped into my bones. You can't celebrate the wonder of Christmas too early for this girl. Matter of fact, Christmas is all about joy and celebration.

My childish exuberance has been passed down to my children and grandchildren. The holiday for our family is steeped in tradition, soaked in laughter, and topped with joy.

It is always over the top, over the money limit, and over the hills, my kids still come back to Grandma's house to experience it.

I cook until I am bone tired. I wrap until my fingers are taped together, and I decorate until the glitter is a permanent feature in my hair.

Celebrating the Christ child should not be about how much trouble Christmas is, but instead, going to the trouble to show someone the joy of loving. Christmas brought us hope, salvation, and genuine pure love covered in swaddling clothes lying on a bed of straw. If I had been there, I would have decorated a tree, wrapped some presents in burlap, and told that new baby Santa was coming!

On a Christmas evening a few years ago, my granddaughter and I were outside watching an unusual sight in Georgia. Huge snowflakes fell softly from the night sky as if they were tiny white lace doily's floating down from heaven.

The porch door opened, and my granddaughter's mother shouted,

"Avery, come in before you catch a cold!"

"But, Mama, it's Christmas!" she yelled, knowing that Christmas would save her from herself.

Christmas is within your heart. Let it shine this holiday season and always.

Merry Christmas, y'all!

The Child Within Us

"Lynn, are you ever going to grow up?" my mother asked as we drove home after my sixty-something birthday celebration.

I have no idea what led up to the question, but I would imagine I was acting completely silly. Silliness and craziness is part of my DNA. Ask anyone who knows me.

"No, Mom, I have no plans of ever doing that. Do I have to?" I replied and then we both started laughing.

I remember making the conscious effort always to have a part of me remain a kid. I did not want to lose what it felt like to run and play, to dream, to imagine, and to laugh out loud. My effort began one day when I was eight years old and waiting for the school bus on the corner across from my house. I, along with several other elementary kids, huddled together in a tight group careful not to stand on the lady's yard next to the bus stop.

She owned the biggest house on the street, and her yard was beautiful. The "Mean Lady" was the only name we knew for her. She lived alone in her quiet rooms without children or laughter. She would scare me to death yelling at the dogs crossing her path and the children chasing after them.

One morning when the fog from the river rose and traveled down our street, a tragedy occurred. My neighbor on the adjacent corner was a sweet little boy with light blond hair and big blue eyes. He had a small, scrappy terrier with a shrill bark that would run like the wind. He loved that crazy little dog and would howl with joy as the terrier chased him.

On that misty morning, the dog left his house to find his buddy. We are not sure how he got out, but when he did, he ran to us from across the street at the same time the bus was coming through the fog.

We watched in horror as the tires hit the little terrier. Desperately injured, the dog battled its way to the Mean Lady's yard. We all ran to him. The scrappy terrier took his last breath while cradled in his little master's arms.

Mean Lady ran from her house when she saw what was happening. We all were in tears, including the bus driver, when Mean Lady yelled at us to get out of her yard. "And, take that old dog with you!" she screamed.

I never forgot that foggy day. It is still so fresh in my mind; tears are now falling down my cheeks as I recall the scene. I believe it was that day when I decided that if growing up meant I would lose what it felt like to be a child, then I never wanted to grow up. Folks who don't remember what it felt like to be a child lose the ability to empathize with the traumas of childhood.

My grandmother was always a kid. She loved playing with children more than adults. My cousins and I thought maybe she didn't have enough toys when she was young, so that is why she liked to play with us. I now understand she made an effort to retain part of her childhood for the children she would love in her life.

When my granddaughter was born, I thought, "Wow, now I have someone to play with!" (No kidding; I did think that.) I wanted to show her how to play with dolls, to dance as if she were on stage, to run in the rain, to laugh until she got hiccups, and to never forget how to enjoy these things.

Christmas for me is a perfect event. Not only do I get to act like a kid legitimately, but I get to thank the good Lord for allowing me to be able to do so. My eyes still sparkle when I see twinkling lights and bright colored ribbon.

There is not one ounce of Bah Humbug in me. I have many

flaws, but Scrooge is no relative of mine.

I have no idea why some folks lose all their child-like behavior. Aren't we all just kids who got older?

When I think of the children who look to an adult and see no sparkle and joy, my heart breaks not only for the child but the adult as well.

This holiday season, perhaps we should all turn back the clock and recall the happiness of our youth when Christmas thrilled us to the point of clapping our hands and dazzled us with wonder. It is probably the best gift we can give to the children we love.

The best gift you can bestow on yourself is to give from your heart to a child who is in need. When you do, you might find yourself laughing out loud and hearing someone say, "Honey, are you ever going to grow up?"

'Twas The Day After Christmas

I think I am still here. I can't feel my feet, and my eyes are about closed, but yes, I just hit myself with the vacuum cleaner, and it hurt! Must mean I am alive after all!

The garbage cans are so full that I am sure my nice trash man will change professions after today. The washing machine is refusing to accept anymore detergent, and the dryer doesn't remember how to stop.

Remnants of Christmas are scattered everywhere along with cookie crumbs and Rice Krispies. Toddler toys are piled high in a child's toy grocery cart, and there is a doll that keeps telling me she loves me when I limp past her.

The Gendusa Family Christmas just happened. Life in our neighborhood may not be the same again. Cars filled the street, the dog ran away, and Jax, my seventeen-month-old grandson, wanted to run folks over with the pink grocery cart that belongs to his little girl cousin. It was amazing how fast he could run from her screams and outstretched arms as she tried to retrieve her cart.

All our blended family, complete with their broods, returned home to celebrate with us. Plus nieces, nephews, and wait, who was that guy? Maybe it was the policeman someone called to the scene of our chaos! I think he decided to eat with us. Not sure.

Today the house is quiet except for the dryer and the vacuum. My children left to visit their Dad in South Carolina, and my husband is exchanging gifts he really liked just to leave the house. I can't believe I am alone! I might take a moment to brush my teeth and hair if I can locate the brushes.

I plan the Gendusa Family Christmas for months. Menus, gifts, desserts, and decorations that resemble some location in the North Pole abound. I realize it gets bigger every year and today, I figured out why.

My oldest grandchild will soon enter her teens. She has always insisted on coming to Grandma's house for the holidays. She adores her cousins and loves the new babies in our brood.

I feel blessed beyond belief that folks still want to come to this winter wonderland I create in celebration. It takes a lot of work to entice this crew, but it has always worked. Now, as the years slip by, I realize there might come a day when the house will be clean on December 26, and no one will need to call the police.

Jax will walk instead of run, and the nephews and nieces will be with their broods in some far away place they call home.

If I could stop time on any given day, it would be on Christmas. I would make each precious second turn into a minute and Christmas day would last another day or two.

However, I know life goes at its own pace. It is something we all must adapt to, but it is still a big adjustment when our lives change. Maybe that is why we have cameras and memory so that we can go back while moving forward.

I take nothing for granted, especially my children. Every day those children, grandchildren, nieces, and nephews are a part of my world, I realize how much God loved me to let me be a part of their lives. What a gift!

When we gather at our table or are laughing, chasing the dog or the babies, or watching Rice Krispies fall from the sky onto the floor, I realize I am happiest amid the chaos.

Yes, one day the Gendusa Family Christmas will not be the same. It will become a memory ingrained into each of those who were blessed to be a part of it.

I hope those who were here will carry it forward to the generations that will follow. One day my soon-to-be teen granddaughter will be watching her soon-to-be teen, recalling Christmastime at Grandma's winter wonderland.

She will tell her child about dinners when we sang the "Twelve Days of Christmas" out of tune and never got it perfect. She will try to explain the games played, the abundance of presents, and the three-tiered, candlelit cake celebrating the birth of Jesus. She will describe the laughter of her parents, her cousins, and babies that made Rice Krispies fall from the sky.

She will tell her child that Christmas is family, it is beautiful, and it is a gift no matter how tired she may be the day after.

The Last Chapter

We all will reach the "last chapter" of our lives. The final page provides an ending for some, but for others, it is a new beginning.

From birth, my life has followed a path leading to a door which has been left ajar for me to enter. The journey has not been without stumbles or falls when shadows produced darkness, and I lost my way.

I was blessed to be able to eventually see the light shining through from the other side of the portal allowing me to find my way back onto the path.

I look forward to the day I view the entire heavenly glory awaiting me beyond the door and start a new chapter of living.

The Beauty Of My "Memory Door"

There is an ugly door next to my desk leading to an unfinished cubby. The door drives me crazy because I usually hit my head on its casing when I try to retrieve something inside the cubby. The door is only five feet tall, so you do have to duck. The duck part and my brain are not always in sync, so I have had a few choice words for the door.

However, even though the door is ugly, there is beauty attached to its sacred back.

I am not sure when I started this, but whenever I attend a person's funeral, I keep the service program. It never seems respectful to throw one away. One day, I hung one on the back of the little door so that I wouldn't lose it. Afterward, I decided to hang them all, and the old white door transformed into my Memory Door. Every time I open it, I am, again, made aware how unique the lives who grace this door indeed were.

Now, this all may sound morbid to some, but to me, it is a comfort. The Memory Door reminds me these fine folks touched lives and made a difference on this earth. It is my little way to honor them.

My brother's program is perfect because it shows three American flags across the front. John's picture is not there, but knowing him, he would rather have the flags. He was a Navy Lieutenant who served his country in Viet Nam. A true American patriot in every sense of the word and a great brother.

My father and mother hang prominently on the door. Their smiling faces captured in a photo taken years ago are alive and well. The picture dates to my teenage years when Dad was in the Rotary Club. The Rotary pin is visible on his lapel. The photograph makes me feel they are forever young, in love, and together as they should be.

Krista Hines Cadenhead was my best friend. We worked together for sixteen years. We could make each other laugh till we were downright silly. Sixteen years of friendship, trust, and love ended way too early when cancer sent her to heaven at age 52. To this day when I do something crazy, I swear I hear her laughter and see her shaking her head in disbelief.

Before Krista left, I promised her I would take her parents the famous Red Velvet cake for Christmas. I had given Krista the recipe years before, and she would bake one for her parents every December. After Krista died, I continued to visit her Mom and Dad during the Holidays bearing the Red Velvet cake.

Several years later, Krista's dad joined her in heaven. What a guy he was! His face is the face of a former baseball player and a loving father. At his service, the minister said, "I never knew a better person than Bob Hines." It has been my privilege and gift to know this family.

Sarah Dye was the loveliest client. She trusted me with every color and every piece of fabric she ever used. She was always so appreciative of my design work for her and such a Godly, talented woman. ALS took Sarah quickly, and the world is not quite as pretty without her. The week before she died she called just to say, "Thank you." However, I was the one blessed by her life.

Jon is the last one on the memory door. At 31, he died suddenly and left a void that nothing can fill. His father is a dear friend, and I keep his picture there to remind me how fragile life can be, how special our children are, and never to take a moment for granted.

These wonderful folks are just a few on my memory board. Their lives still live on with God. Faith teaches us that we will meet up with those we love again in a place where there will be no more funerals, no more programs, no more tears, and no need for a memory door.

Until then, I use my door to see Bob and hope heaven has Red Velvet cakes and a baseball field. I notice Krista laughing and hear her beautiful voice singing a hymn. I envision Sarah begging me to paint this door so it will be prettier. I can see my brother in his Navy splendor saluting the flags, and my parents cringing when I use those words on the door when I don't duck.

Finally, I see Jon with his happy face and beautiful spirit reminding us all is well and beautiful in the heavenly life beyond the door.

"For God so loved the world, that he gave his only begotten Son, that whosoever believeth in Him should not perish, but shall have everlasting life."

John 3:16

Elizabeth & Ray Walker circa 1965

Life, Death And "S" Hooks

There are many books, testimonials, and arguments about life after death. There will always be theories regarding heaven and hell, and whether there is a God or not. It is my sincere belief there is a God and life after death. I was taught to believe in both, but I am confirmed in my faith by things I have witnessed in life. This truth became apparent by a wickedly funny brother and "S" hooks.

How many people have you heard say their dearly departed mother, brother or sister talked to them in a dream or a room?

You ask some of these same folks, and they are still unsure Heaven exists. Skeptical, cynical, scared; who knows why. I can tell you one thing for sure; death will happen.

It happened to my brother. John received a diagnosis of terminal cancer at the age of fifty-two. He was almost seven years older and always seventy years smarter than I was, an engineer, a lover of all things political, and dedicated to his beloved Navy. A Vietnam veteran, a father of two, a defender and protector of his only sister. He and I were about as different as molasses and vinegar, but we loved one another immensely.

Before my brother died after a three-year illness, he was not able to walk. He would sit in his big recliner, look out the window and watch the redbirds eating seed out of the bird feeder. He would laugh at how they would vie for food, flutter their wings and spread their silly joy into his space.

I don't remember John enjoying watching birds before his illness, but when life's door is closing, I would think you are desperately searching for earthly living treasures. Things that have been there all along the way, but suddenly you notice them now as little gifts to ease your burdens.

In the early hours of an April morning, John Walker took his last breath. In some corner of my mind, I can envision the red birds accompanying his flight toward heaven.

Once I returned to work after his death, my friends gave me a birdhouse. "We wanted to give you something you would treasure to remember his love." A wonderful gift.

A few weeks passed and one Saturday I decided it was time to hang my birdhouse. It resembled an old wood-sided, rustic country home. A magnificent Japanese magnolia was next to my rocking chair front porch. It was the perfect place for the birdhouse to hang.

I went to the garage to get a chain and an "S" hook to attach the house from a limb of the tree. I owned a workbench, with pegboard above to hang tools from, and little cubbies for tacks, nails, brads, screws, etc., including "S" hooks.

To my frustration, I could not find the "S" hooks! All I needed was one, and I knew they were there!!

"I am not going to Home Depot for one "S" hook," I yelled!

"John, if you want me to hang this birdfeeder, then tell me where the hooks are!"

Suddenly, I felt something fall on top of my feet. My feet were near the bottom shelf of the workbench where I stored old tools and a few baskets.

A basket had fallen on my foot, but I had not touched the shelf. The basket was brimming with "S" hooks. About fifty or more were now all over the floor and on top of my feet.

For a moment, I went silent, then I laughed. If I tell you that was my brother, THAT was my brother! He knew I would have to pick up all fifty to get one! I could hear his laughter mixed with my own, plus I understood he was alive and still full of wicked humor.

The years passed and every spring I would ask my best friend and coworker, Krista, what day my brother died. She would reply, "April 29th". I asked her so many times she finally wrote it down for me.

"I don't know why I can't remember the date!" I would exclaim.

Later Krista died at fifty-two from cancer, and a pure joy left this earth. As I sat in the church to bid her farewell, tears streamed down my face. I opened her program, and because grief is consuming, I had not realized that she went to Heaven's welcoming arms on April 29th.

She knew I would never forget the date again.

You may believe all of this is a coincidence, a mystery. I say it's God whispering to us that life and laughter continue beyond Heaven's door.

When Love Leaves

John Harrison Smith was my first crush. Our Dads worked together at the lumber mill, and on Sundays after church we would go to the mill and ride on the forklifts. John and I were both only ten years old.

I still have the straw-stuffed, red and white bear he won at the fair for me all those years ago. Never had the heart to throw it away. John was also the provider of my first kiss.

One day, in 9th grade, John Smith developed a crush on another girl, and then he was gone. It was my first time to feel a crack in my innocent heart.

My family would move to another state by 10th grade, and I never saw my first love again.

Hearts break every minute of every day somewhere. We never are prepared, we are never going to understand why entirely, and we will never heal the pain by ourselves.

We don't like to talk about our emotions too much, but the truth is, love leaving can sometimes plant the seed for depression, suicide, physical ailments, and, yes, even murder. A broken heart can lead to a broken person. However, whether love left because of death or divorce, there is the help to heal.

We call our friends, counselors, and family to come to our aid. Without their support and understanding, the pain would be worse. However, they are not there in the quiet moments when the mind collapses, and sleep is impossible.

On a hot summer day in August of 1965, my Grandmother was putting the finishing touches on lunch. Cornbread, beans, buttermilk, and tomatoes from the garden spread over the table. As usual, she sent Snowball, their dog, to get my Grandfather at his mill across the pond when lunch was ready.

Snowball would run to the mill and then leisurely stroll down the path home with her master by her side.

Laughing as he came through the door, Granddaddy left to wash his hands in the powder room next to the kitchen. He never returned.

A fatal heart attack killed him so swiftly that my Grandmother never even heard a whimper.

Her sweet love suddenly was gone, leaving my Grandmother devastated.

She would live another twenty-four years always loving her husband, and after a while, her laughter returned and blessed our lives forever. The pain did not define her because, at some point, she had handed the pain to God.

Another woman I know went on a trip one day with girlfriends. When she returned from her vacation, her husband of thirty years had vanished. Divorce would follow along with bitterness, anger, and resentment raging within her soul. But, it didn't stay.

After a few months, she started helping others in need and forgave the man who deserted her. Her anger and resentment didn't define her; instead, at some point, she handed her bitterness to God.

These two women still grieved. They continued a daily effort of putting one foot in front of the other healing with every step. But if you were to ask them today, in the end, what eased their burden, they simply replied, "God."

Many years ago I was suffering from the intense pain of a broken heart. I tried and tried to mend it, but there was nothing I could do to cure the heartache. Love was gone.

On a particularly dark and lonely night, I lay in my bed but instead of sleeping, tossed and turned. With only a street light illuminating my room, I saw the old straw-stuffed bear on a shelf, the soft light landing on his big, brown eyes.

I got up, pulled him off the shelf and fell to my knees. I

prayed so hard and cried so much that my bear's fur was left damp. When I opened my eyes, I noticed the street light cast a shadow through the window panes creating a perfect cross on my wall.

In my darkest hour, I had found the light of God.

It was God's love which always got me through the many heartaches that would come in my life. To this day, I am thankful for the young man whose love left.

I know an excellent cardiologist. If Dr. Sandler told me tomorrow I would have to take twenty pills a day to cure a physical heart issue, I would. I TRUST him to care for me, to use his expertise to heal me. He and I would do everything we could to get the most living out of my life.

Dr. Sandler, however, as good as he is, cannot repair the broken heart. He cannot see the anger, resentment, pain, or loneliness created by a lost love.

If you are experiencing a broken heart that is slow to heal or if resentment has consumed you, try grabbing a stuffed bear, hold on to him tight, fall on your knees, and let the Great Healer start to mend you. TRUST Him just like you do your doctor.

His curing prescription is, "Come to Me, all you weary and heavy laden, and I will give you rest." Soon light will shine through your soul. The good news is: His love will never leave.

Not Even Death Can Stop Their Music

Elizabeth "Teenie" Kerr died this past weekend in South Carolina at the age of ninety-eight. Her son, Rick, and his wife, Deborah are our close friends and live next door.

Like Teenie, my mother, Elizabeth, was born in 1919, but she passed away seven years before Rick's mother. Both women were strong willed and independent. Both loved their husbands, family, friends, and the game of bridge.

Teenie and Mom didn't meet until they were both approaching ninety. When I discovered Teenie was coming to visit Rick and Deborah, I decided it was time for these girls to meet. I arranged a luncheon for them plus two of Mom's friends so they could enjoy a bridge game afterwards.

It was a magical spring day when these four lunched under the branches of an oak tree as a warm breeze stirred the flowers adorning the table. These octogenarians cackled like young girls while sharing stories and learning they all lived similar lives. They played serious bridge until the late afternoon and when they waved goodbye I caught a glimpse of sadness in their eyes.

When I learned of Teenie's death, I realized all the ladies who met under the oak tree on that lovely spring day were now gone. There would be no more challenging bridge games, no more special luncheons, and I would never again hear the joyful cackling these four produced.

As I was lying on the sofa the Sunday night after Teenie died, I recalled every detail of that special day. I longed to hear my parents' laughter one more time. Daddy's belly shook when he laughed, and Mama would sometimes bend over grabbing her knees if she got tickled. I would love to see Teenie, who walked as if she were trying to stomp the earth under her feet, tromp toward me.

My mind was lost in the memory of those I longed to see when my phone dinged with a message from niece, Emily. She had found a video about another spring day in 1999 and sent it to me.

The video was of my old house in Roswell which sat on a hill with steps that led precariously up to its big rocking chair front porch.

It was April 9th and the day of my parents 60th wedding anniversary. We had planned a surprise party for them and invited many folks from the independent senior living facility where they had resided for two years.

I rented a small bus to bring their neighbors to my home where a feast awaited them. It took many strapping young men to escort these elderly folks up to the porch and through the doors. Some with walkers and others with canes ambled in with enormous smiles on their faces as they saw the party atmosphere.

When my parents arrived, yells of "Surprise!" shocked them. Faces of grandchildren, family, and old friends greeted them. My Dad looked confused and then started belly laughing. Mom bent over and grabbed her knees. Laughter, hugs, and joy filled the entire house.

The video showed the moments when mom and dad cut the buttercream frosted three-tiered cake. People gathered around the table to fill their plates and smell the roses adorning the dining room. The cameras clicked, and glasses clinked as the sounds of Guy Lombardo's band swayed the room.

Old stories were brought to life as youth filled the hearts of those spry, senior folks on that spring day when the dogwoods were erupting, and tulips graced the lawns.

As I continued to pour over every detail of the video, I saw my mother as I would like always to remember her. She was radiant and beautiful. At 80, she still had naturally dark hair with little gray, and she could walk those stairs without a hand. She was amazing. Dad was still laughing and could tell a joke or story that could make a room roar.

Seven months after the party, Dad's stories and laughter were silenced. He had given my mother sixty years of love.

When I first started watching the film of that day in 1999 unfold, I got a lump in my throat and a tear in my eye; I was so sad.

Then I realized God had just sent me a special gift. He had brought my parents right back into my living room! Their voices and laughter filled the air and joy sprang into my heart.

No longer did I see death, but rather living. No longer did I have a tear in my eye, but instead a smile on my face.

I realized Daddy is still telling stories and Mom's wise counsel and steady hands are still used to guide her family's way.

Death is just a door we go through. I believe if I peeked through it today I might catch a glimpse of Teenie Kerr playing a round of bridge with mama and cackling with old friends. I probably would spot Daddy telling his funny tales to a room full of folks while Guy Lombardo and his band play on.

I dedicate this story to the many from the Greatest Generation who have left us. May your love, your laughter, and your courage never be forgotten. May your music always play on.

"Well Done, My Good And Faithful Servant!"

He was born in 1908 in a small Tennessee town in the mountains. By the time he was twelve, his father had passed away, and he had become the big brother as well as a mentor to his three siblings. However, Paul Walker always had a dream: He wanted to become a physician.

William Fackler was born in 1920 in a small Georgia community outside Macon. Bright, determined and ready to make a difference in the world, he left for Emory to fulfill a dream: He wanted to become a physician.

Paul Walker became a surgeon, and William Fackler became an internist and cardiologist.

Uncle Paul was a huge part of my life as a young girl. I was a sickly little one and when he came to visit, he would always try to help but become discouraged when there wasn't an easy solution to the asthma and other allergies that plagued me. Paul Walker was a great physician and surgeon, but in my eyes, he was my uncle whom I not only respected, but dearly loved.

By the time we moved to LaGrange from Tennessee in 1962, my Uncle Paul was the Medical Director of the United States Public Health Service and living in New York.

Dr. Fackler lived across the street from where we built our home in LaGrange. His children went to school with me and became friends. Long before we were neighbors, he had established himself as one of the most exceptional physicians and men in LaGrange.

It was September 1963 when I became ill. After school, I left to play basketball with the guys down my street, and for some reason, the ball just couldn't reach the basket. My famous long shot was woefully short.

"Mom, I can't hit the basket!" I screamed as I walked through the door.

She immediately put her hand on my forehead.

"You have a bit of a fever; I'll make an appointment with a doctor." After the visit, the diagnosis was the flu.

By Christmas the same year I was still not well, experiencing high fevers and complete energy depletion. Mom made another appointment with a different doctor, our new neighbor, Dr. Fackler.

"You are a sick girl!" he said with a slight smile knowing that was apparent, which made me chuckle. I noticed a concerned look on his face when he found my spleen so swollen I couldn't fasten my skirt, and it took all I could do to stand.

"You have mononucleosis which is bordering on hepatitis," Dr. Fackler explained. "My guess is you have been sick for months, and now we have some hurdles to cross. You are going to need to follow my instructions exactly," he stated sternly while looking into my eyes, so I understood he meant business.

Afterward, Dr. Fackler became our family doctor.

Once I married, my husband and I lived in a tiny home near the hospital. One Sunday morning I awoke with a terrible headache. By late afternoon, my eyesight became blurred, and I could no longer see color.

My husband called my Dad; my Dad called Dr. Fackler. A short time later the good doctor was standing at our door with his black bag in hand.

As he sat at the foot of my bed, I witnessed the same concerned look which he exhibited many times before. When he opened his bag after a quick exam, he retrieved a horrific looking instrument I could barely see.

"Why do you have a horse syringe?" I asked, squinting.

"I carry one just for you!" he joked.

After the horse serum injection, he waited until I fell asleep.

Before leaving, he explained to my husband that I was experiencing my first migraine.

I was living in Birmingham in the early 70s when my life started to unravel. I drove home one weekend to visit Mom and Dad who knew I was struggling. When I walked through my parent's door, Dad proclaimed, "You have an appointment with Dr. Fackler today."

"Dad, what can Dr. Fackler do for me? He can't stop the crying or the heartache. Besides, it's Saturday, and I don't want to bother him!"

"He is waiting for you!" my Dad insisted.

I walked into Dr. Fackler's office with tear-stained cheeks. After a heartfelt hug, I sat across from him and again, noticed the same concerned face I had grown to love over the years.

Gentle words, kindness, understanding, and empathy were exchanged between a doctor and his patient. He talked for as long as words were necessary to be said. He took all the time needed for me on a Saturday when he probably craved time for himself.

I wish I could have the whole page of this paper to tell all the stories, but I am just one of so many lives this good and noble man touched with his care and commitment to healing.

When Uncle Paul retired from the Public Health service, he was able to start a lucrative private practice anywhere in the country. Instead, Paul Walker recruited other physicians to establish a medical clinic on the border of Kentucky and West Virginia to aid the most impoverished people in America.

Upon his death, we received letters not only from the governor of West Virginia, but from many former patients and friends. Our family learned of all the work he had done for others, not only in service to his country, but for the citizens of West Virginia, his church, and his family. His altruism and love for those in need was his gift and he used it well.

These two men were exceptional children of God who lived

very similar lives and who realized early they were born for service to heal the sick and the broken. Two young men had a dream to become physicians. We will never know exactly how many lives they touched, but I know God kept a record. I would love to see that number.

These highly regarded gentlemen left a mark on this earth with their gift of intelligence combined with loving hearts. They not only cured the ill but held the hands of those suffering.

I am sure Dr. William Byron Fackler and Dr. Paul Eugene Walker heard the same sentence when they each walked through heaven's door.

"Well done, my good and faithful servant."

Dr. Paul Eugene Walker
1906-1979

Dr. William Byron Fackler, Jr.
1920-2018

My Prayer

Dear Lord,

When I feel there is no one to love me
Help me to remember that you "unconditionally" do.

When there is no one to invite me to share a meal
Help me to remember your last meal was served for me.

When there is no one to talk to
Help me to listen for your voice whispering in my ear.

When I feel there is little hope to live
Help me to remember that you died to give me hope.

When I feel I am losing a fight with Satan
Help me to remember that you have already won the battle.

When my tears won't dry, and my heart won't stop aching
Help me to remember that when I cry, so do you.

When my unforgiving nature raises its ugly head
Help me to remember that in your last painful hour, you
raised your head and said, "Forgive."

And, Lord, when I don't understand why I don't get my way
Help me to remember that you are the truth, the light, and the
only way.

Help me to remember.
Amen.

About the Author

After spending forty-three years as an Interior Designer, Lynn Walker Gendusa was ready to retire to a hammock somewhere overlooking the blue ocean.

Except, God had other plans. Within a few weeks of putting down her tape measure, she picked up a pen. Her first story was published in the *LaGrange Daily News* in LaGrange, Georgia, her former hometown. Within a few more weeks, she became a weekly columnist for the paper, writing essays about faith, America, family, friends, depression, joy, holidays, and the other stuff of life.

Her work soon spread across the country to other publications that loved her relatable down-home stories that are laced with inspiration as well as frankness.

Lynn has compiled many of her columns into these pages after readers encouraged her to do so. Her mission is to always inspire and remind us of life's abundant blessings.

She believes, "Every day reveals a new story, a new bend in the road, and a clearer understanding of our journey."

Lynn currently resides in Roswell, Georgia with her husband David. She is the mother of three grown children, two stepchildren, and three grandchildren.

Lynn can be reached at lynnwalkergendusa@gmail.com and on Facebook as Lynn Walker Gendusa. Her columns continue weekly and can be read on line at lagrangenews.com.